Double Bind

D0920716

Double Bind — Rhea Anastas and Leigh Ledare

A.R.T. Press

In this book Leigh Ledare and I view his body of work *Double Bind* to audition ideas about social and aesthetic experience within the unfolding of a dialogue.[1] The prolific imagery of *Double Bind*—its just under one thousand photographs, and its collection of mass-media ephemera—confronts the viewer in the work's physical installation in single images (as framed photographs), pairs or sequences of visual materials (of which "montages" and diptychs are elements), and en masse in three table-top vitrines (as large arrangements of stacked photos and varied ephemera). *Double Bind* enacts recognizable subjects in this space: the male-female vessel of intimacy that we know as the heterosexual couple. Ledare's work seizes upon familiarity with marital relations and at the same time disorients the familiar, as I face (and you and we face) conflicting scales of subjectivity (of multiple viewers, of the work's participant-performers). Sexuality and intimacy, or the surfaces of sexuality and intimacy that it may be possible to make visible, are posed and tested again and again by the work's performances and camera-based and appropriated images. To ask questions about viewing the material and social ensemble of *Double Bind* is to think within the contradictions of the cultural, psychological, and sexual realms. The texts of this book intervene within and extend the social and aesthetic poiesis of the work.[2] Our conversation also becomes an occasion to attempt concepts that depart from critical practices of recent decades. Just as *Double Bind* pivots from assumptions about physical sight and its deconstruction as the ordering principle of subject/object and self/other, toward an identificatory complexity and a varied phenomena of experience and the body, we disengage from the usual critical habits that give language ontological primacy. In this way, the book *Double Bind* tests a concept of affective criticism by *doing*, modeling responses created for and within the different scales—both intimate, and public or collective—of artwork and viewership.

Ledare created *Double Bind* over 2009–2010, making use of a select set of social facts from his lived experience. Ledare's idea was to temporarily rearrange the relations of a couple by placing himself and his former partner in marriage together as a both real and performed element within the work's structure. During the summer of 2009, with this concept in place, Ledare asked Meghan Ledare-Fedderly (a clothing designer, for five years divorced from Ledare), to spend a weekend with him at a cabin in upstate New York and to participate in photography for the work during the trip. What we see of this encounter in *Double Bind* are close to five hundred black-and-white photographs, prints of every exposure on the fourteen rolls of film that Ledare shot over the three days. In parallel, Ledare-Fedderly returned to the same cabin in September 2009 with Adam Fedderly (a photographer, and her new husband) at Ledare's invitation. Meghan and Adam also produced photographs over their three-day stay, handing their film over to Ledare, who printed every exposure of Fedderly's many film rolls as well, totaling slightly under one thousand combined photos from both trips. Later, during the fall–winter of 2009–2010, while living and working between Los Angeles and New York, Ledare produced the other elements of *Double Bind*: a print-media collection of some six thousand pages appropriated from a wide range of magazines, newspapers, and other periodicals, and forty-eight panels of imagery that arranged and montaged his and Fedderly's photographs with these mass-media materials.

The work's three participants carry out private performances that enact their lived experience within contemporary aesthetics, as well as within the transformed spheres of identity and sexuality in the present—after the events of the civil rights, sexual revolution, and gay-liberation movements, and later the AIDS epidemic and the xenophobic and homophobic controls of Reagan-Bush-Clinton-Bush-era American and global policies. Culture and identity, as narrative or archetype or advertisement or service, literally materialize in *Double Bind*'s collection of mass-cultural media. In *Double Bind* this imagery—as representation, as spectacle— complexly coexists with the situational and contingent social encounters of its participants; the two layers are married and compared, they separate and clash. What does *Double Bind* want to show us about the sexuality it may only partially display in its photographed encounters? Viewers of the work, both visually and projectively, experience the participants' experiences—in some fragmentary and artificial but still intimate way. Since

Double Bind emanates from within Ledare's private relationships and background, the ideas he culled are lived, and theorized out of informal, self-organized thinking. In the dialogue, we consider concepts of enactment and complicity. Such descriptions of identificatory complexity gain in recognition within the problematics of a "subjectivity of negativity," to name a cluster of very recent definitions and debates about subjectification that bridge the present moment and earlier feminist negativities.[3] We approach this viewing of looks and projections as an affective field of visual-bodily contact, reaction, and counterreaction. When I view, when Ledare views, when you view, and when we view (all of us who inhabit the work's space and that of other, similar social life), which responses can be attributed to experience, to sight or touch or feeling, to belief or ideology? Which responses are granted strong functions as concepts and working theories?[4] This book attends to *Double Bind*'s concepts as cultural, and yet does this from the viewpoints of materiality and psychology—and from intimacy, if intimacy can be a viewpoint—giving visibility to and elevating fields of informal and self-organized expression.

The dialogue's questions about sexuality and culture issue from a tradition of feminist critical stances toward knowledge, which Teresa de Lauretis has written about as an unauthorized and disobedient relationship to the symbolic order, as women's emptied-out relation to this order (a relation that may be assumed by anyone who recognizes that feminism is in his or her interest).[5] Feminism acted and wrote into and against phallogocentric knowledge, enabling new forms of social life. As Ledare and I talked, we gathered a set of artworks, books, and essays that became models for us, and which we drew on in the course of dialoguing. We entered feminist discourse from what felt like a new point on an old and familiar map of ideas, the critiques of the Milan Women's Bookstore Collective of the 1970s onward, and this group's connections and conceptual parallels to Luce Irigaray's critiques of philosophy. In the mid-1980s, Italian feminist Adriana Cavarero wrote: "The task of thinking sexual difference is thus an arduous one because sexual difference lies precisely in the erasure on which Western philosophy has been founded and developed. To think sexual difference starting from the male universal is to think it as already thought, that is, to think it through the categories of a thought that is supported by the non-thinking of difference itself."[6] Traditional aesthetics assumes a universalism of forms or subjects. We know this setup is a moral superiority, and a racial and sexual one, fixing claims about identities by means of transhistorical descriptive languages and stabilized viewing positions. Marriage is among the everyday forms of patriarchy that feminism as a theory and social practice has, more than any other political or social institution, cast out of conventionality and pushed into a space of open questioning. For us, these feminist expressions of disobedience in the face of such preconstituted, socially typed relations express negativity—*your world, I don't want it!*—and powerfully invert the status quo of thought and action. In the context of *Double Bind*'s imagery, Samuel Delany's description of the exclusive, monogamous conditions of heterosexual coupling as "only a particular form of a *socially prescribed perversion*" was essential to us in seeing and resisting the symbolic controls of gender in and around marriage.[7] The argument against the gay-marriage movement within queer activism and thought today also negates in a similar fashion, resting on a refusal of the binary choices of equality-based arguments (e.g., yes/no to gay marriage) as these choices are offered by electoral politics.[8]

I can't imagine attending to my own responses to *Double Bind*'s repetitive imagery of Meghan or to the work's media collection— its page after torn page of bodies and gazes in advertisements, editorial layouts, and pornography—without the feminist critique of sexual difference. Is the photography and print media of *Double Bind* an imagery of sexual difference? This continuous line of questioning structures the dialogue. Still, the feminist critique of sexual difference is not a tool or set of formulations that Ledare and I are willing to set forth as true or stable or use exclusively. Can I view, and continue to view, *Double Bind* with feminist eyes that hold the creation of exceptional-woman and idealized-feminine imagery as prohibited, for the reason that it may not have women's best interests in mind? Can I say that Meghan is naked or clothed for herself? Or for Ledare, for Fedderly, for other men? In asking these questions, I worry about the social typing they perform, the assumptions about the expropriation of female sexual significations and the appropriations of white-male privilege that connect to this directionality.[9] Are the politics of these questions coming across clearly as Leigh and I pose them and you read them in the present day? When Ledare-Fedderly is photographed, at times embodying and throwing off these sexual potencies, what effects are there to sort through, to be excited by or to feel cautious about? What effects may she be having on herself, on others, or on our reception of images and our languages for viewing? Bound up with these raw speculations are the relational roles of Leigh, Meghan, and Adam. How is Ledare actually using Meghan's potencies? What are the effects of his complex framings of the performers' expressions as social materials, as vehicles for this artwork and its viewers?

In Eve Kosofsky Sedgwick's 2003 volume *Touching Feeling: Affect, Pedagogy, Performativity*, Sedgwick reflects on the limits of reading through sexual-difference theory. To perform analyses according to feminist critiques can mean applying the logic of cause and effect. Sedgwick doesn't want to devalue (in her very apt wording) the tradition of these critiques, but rather "to explore some ways around the topos of depth or hiddenness, typically followed by a drama of exposure, that has been such a staple of critical work of the past four decades."[10] In this dialogue we recognize and honor the potentials of thinking in continuity with the feminist critique of the ocular and its violent history for gendered and sexual identities, but we search out techniques that, like Sedgwick's, are less directional. The acts of entering and internalization, expropriation and articulation, that play out in *Double Bind* as contingencies and complicities are acts, behaviors, and cognitions within the work's dynamics of participation. Ledare describes the structure for *Double Bind* this way: "*Double Bind*'s triangulated relationships cast photography's function as multiple: as a catalyst for the performance of self-expression; as communicating and reproducing through individual subjects an existing symbolic system; and finally as a feedback mechanism that might allow us a vantage from which to observe our involvement within the interrelation of these functions."[11] How is photography in Ledare's hands not merely representational, but inclusive of what Sedgwick recognizes as ecological or systemic functions—to reiterate Ledare, as catalyst, communication, and feedback? How are nonphotographic and nonverbal qualities rematerialized or reapproached through *Double Bind*'s spatial thinking? This pivoting from temporalization into spatialization, and the application of an affective approach to sexual life and aesthetic critique, bring *Double Bind* into alignment with some of the questions posed by Sedgwick's study. In *Double Bind* and in this book, Ledare searches out how photography and the ocular may be transformed by practices and concepts derived from outside their purview.

Double Bind asks us to think within the cultural formations of identity and social typing; of sexuality, mass media, and history; of fantasy and language or structure. So, in my work as a feminist scholar and in my everyday experience, I find myself caught in a dilemma, knotted up by viewing and feeling uncertain about the value of some of what received feminist theoretical approaches assume: the desexed prohibitions on fantasy and pleasure of sexual difference critiques; and the dualistic, positivistic notion that there *can* exist a progressive, nonsexist imagery of heterosexual relations. I am unsteady in the roles of writer and receiver of this work—but in the process of viewing, I gain in scope when I hold the complexities of my identifications and their negative force close. This is my substance as a viewer, which *is* something thicker than the virtual and distanced position of the critic; my orientation toward the work is complicit with it. Ledare writes about viewing *Double Bind*: "the subject is forced to reconcile [a] strangeness, not in sight of the other but, leading circuitously through the other, to themselves."[12] *Double Bind* may have the effect—an effect feminist critiques also have—of returning knowledge and seeing to us as conjoined problems. My own bind is to work through this, to drench the writing in this dynamic of responsibility and sensory excess, in this strangeness (of self and/in other) and its negative or inverted conditions.

During the months that followed my first viewing of *Double Bind* in Los Angeles in March 2012, Ledare and I began having conversations and writing e-mails. Our exchange continued without any goal in mind for about a year and a half. The idea of writing something together had not yet arisen. By fall 2013, Ledare was planning to exhibit *Double Bind* at Mitchell-Innes & Nash in New York. It was this exhibition that led to our decision to formalize our dialogue, and to then make decisions about the articulation, motivations, and structure of our project.

It may surprise readers that I haven't sought to make distinctions by continually locating Ledare as an artist and myself as a viewer or scholar. We don't think much of identities fashioned into set roles (and the attendant anxieties about mastery in fixing or naming these), or believe assumptions about the split nature of the labor of artists and writers. In fact, "special access," as intimate work between a writer and artist is usually represented, is for authors a claim of status and ownership, and for artists a claim of privilege about who gains access to them. This book's dialogue refutes this mode of thinking about artist-writer collaboration. Our techniques reach for the contingencies of viewing and the recording of those dynamics in language, at every turn pointing to the gaps that lie between work and receiver, work and interpretation.

This book-length dialogue (which nears, but is not precisely a monograph) advances through a series of deliberate, repeated acts of viewing and talking about viewing. Its six sections have been divided based upon the conversation's arc and a loose ordering of its concepts, both in service of continually asking: What happens inside this piece? What else do I have to think about, listen to, read, or see? As Fred Moten writes, "Form is what emerges from the informal."[13] The point here is to take the responsibilities of performing and receiving *Double Bind*, and in other artwork engaged in similar investigations or interventions, seriously. Can art writing be unsparing about what doesn't feel good, what shames as well as what gives pleasure—which is to say, can it be forthright about the intensities and the visceral things that happen during viewing? What does collaborating do to shape this viewing, to heighten these intensities? The multiplicity and mutability of being within *Double Bind* is the noise of sensory excess: call it the viewer's viewing aloud. Being in the world with some amount of self-implication, out in the open, may bring me closer to the capacities of an ethically responsible position. My notion of *Double Bind*'s relations of looking, my acts of locating them in language, record my irritation, my pleasure, and my uncertain states and senses in cognition and viewing. As ideas and terms accumulate and separate and make friction, the dialogue as a form can be open to one and to others.

1.   The book's coauthored dialogue was produced by taping conversations and then developing the ideas and composing the language from the transcribed dialogue as a work of coproduced, collaborative writing. Ledare and I recorded conversations on January 28, 2014 in Los Angeles, and on February 4, 6, and 7, 2014 in New York. Viewing *Double Bind* as Ledare installed it at Mitchell-Innes & Nash in New York on April 11 and 14, 2014 was crucial to developing the transcript into a structured manuscript that possessed conceptual and palpable connections to the installed work. The close viewing of individual photographs and panels we draw from in section II was completed in the presence of these objects within the exhibition. Our editing process continued over multiple rounds of discussion and commenting, balancing the conceptual space of this type of shared and debated thinking and exchanging with the dialogue's quality of featuring two distinct voices (both aspects which differ from a single author's style of address).

2.   Within a spectrum of diverse uses of the concept and word *poiesis*, I will point the reader to a lucid one from an interview with Sylvia Wynter, as paraphrased by her interviewers from Wynter's 1976 talk "Ethno or Socio Poetics": "You say [in "Ethno or Socio Poetics"] that poetics or *poiesis* is so important not as some narrow, literary affair but because it tends to signify all these repressed or stigmatized orders of cognition, ones which differ profoundly from our now orthodox, linear modes of thinking or theorizing" (34). "ProudFlesh Inter/Views: Sylvia Wynter," in *ProudFlesh: New Afrikan Journal of Culture, Politics and Consciousness* 4 (2006): 1–35.

3.   On the "subjectivity of negativity," I want to think with Stefano Harney and Fred Moten's concepts of the general antagonism, study, and informality. "The general antagonism" captures forms of social life and aesthetic critique and, as I see it, takes up social life in ways that claims-based art history and critical writing, with its masteries and pessimisms, puts aside. Harney and Moten's collaboration issues from a black-radical tradition that refuses society's frameworks, norms, and xenophobia. The negativity in Harney and Moten's concept of subjectivity holds out against collectivity. The commitment to a language of social life and to expanding what gets counted as intellectual thought comes forward in concrete socialities, as well as in their coproduced critical model—the model itself enacts the ideas. Harney and Moten's thinking encompasses feminist critiques (such as those of the Milan Women's Bookstore Collective), and overlaps with current debates about negativity in queer theory. See Stefano Harney and Fred Moten, *The Undercommons: Fugitive Planning & Black Study* (New York: Minor Compositions, 2013).

4.   I use "strong theory" after Eve Kosofsky Sedgwick's language of "strong" and "weak" theory, based on her study of Silvan Tomkins and his concepts of theory within affect drives. See Eve Kosofsky Sedgwick, *Touching Feeling: Affect, Pedagogy, Performativity* (Durham & London: Duke University Press, 2003).

5.   Teresa de Lauretis, "The Practice of Sexual Difference and Feminist Thought in Italy: An Introductory Essay," in The Milan Women's Bookstore Collective, *Sexual Difference: A Theory of Social-Symbolic Practice*, ed. Teresa de Lauretis, trans. Teresa de Lauretis and Patricia Cicogna (Bloomington and Indianapolis: Indiana University Press, 1990), 1–21.

6.   Adriana Cavarero, quoted in de Lauretis, "The Practice of Sexual Difference and Feminist Thought in Italy," 4.

7.   Samuel Delany, "Aversion/Perversion/Diversion," in *Longer Views: Extended Essays* (Hanover and London: Wesleyan University Press, 1996), 141; emphasis mine.

8.   See Jack Halberstam, "The Wild Beyond: With and for the Undercommons," introduction to Harney and Moten, *The Undercommons*, 5–12; see, in particular, 8. For a recent queer polemic against gay marriage, see also Bruce Benderson, *Against Marriage* (Los Angeles: Semiotext(e), 2014). Benderson's essay was one of twenty-eight pamphlets produced by Semiotext(e) as part of its contribution to the 2014 Whitney Biennial.

9.   This directional condition as it enacts white-male privilege can be richly connected to the economic foundations of Western Euroethnic bourgeois models where patriarchy and capitalism adhere: what Sylvia Wynter refers to as "homo oeconomicus (the virtuous breadwinner, the stable job holder, the taxpayer, the savvy investor, the master of natural scarcity)" (19). Sylvia Wynter and Katherine McKittrick, "Unparalleled Catastrophe for Our Species? Or, to Give Humanness a Different Future: Conversations," in *Sylvia Wynter: On Being Human as Praxis*, ed. Katherine McKittrick (Durham & London: Duke University Press, 2015), 9–89.

10.   Sedgwick, *Touching Feeling*, 8. This "drama of exposure" is Sedgwick's description of the process and authority of the critic in the name of progressive critical practices, whose sexual-difference tools fall into what she terms "applied theory" (93–94). See, particularly, Sedgwick's introduction (1–25), and also the essay "Paranoid Reading and Reparative Reading, or, You're So Paranoid, You Probably Think This Essay Is About You" (123–151).

11.   Page 46–47.

12.   Page 245.

13.   Harney and Moten, *The Undercommons*, 128. Moten dialogues about Marvin Gaye's song "What's Going On?" and its talk-filled beginning as manifesting the idea of study and this openness and creativity of informality. Moten points out that the song includes meaningful traces of its recording session, a negative ("nothing") mark of study, of this theory of informality that is the subject of his and Harney's book.

They are playing a game. They are playing at not playing a game. If I show them
I see they are, I shall break the rules and they will punish me. I must play their game,
of not seeing I see the game.
            —R. D. Laing, *Knots*

The social order may only ever reluctantly reveal to us how its
meanings *mean*, and how we figure into its circuit of meaning-
making. While permitted to play certain roles, we each realize,
nevertheless, that we face restrictions on how we may perform
ourselves—constraints around gender, class, family, marriage, and
education all come to mind. Moreover, we're aware of other roles
from which we're prohibited: being me exempts me from being
someone I am not. This overlaying of intersubjective relations
(and attempts to conserve their fixity) underwrites the social.
Reciprocating these contracts, we interpolate them only to impose
them on others. If others don't play their roles, how then can we
play ours? Threatened by disorder, we tend to cast it as antisocial.
We fence off disorder in order to separate *it* from *us*, scrutinizing
and confining it, or disregarding it altogether. Similarly, we take
pains to regulate the *it* in *us*. This splitting takes maintenance.

Double Bind consciously embodies these mechanisms, enacting
an analog of our social system and its dynamics—the purpose
being to map it, to splay it out, to let things emerge which exceed
this ordering so as to disorder it. As such, the conceptual rubric
underlying *Double Bind* serves as a container to hold contradiction,
siting its participants as well as its viewer amidst—and between—a
set of conflicting and irresolvable demands. Slipping between
performance and reality, the subjects of *Double Bind* are drawn
into a highly self-reflexive space of acting out, being acted upon,
and reflecting over their own complicity. In this sense, *Double
Bind* is both written out of, and performs a writing-back into, the
earlier reception of my work.

The materials of *Double Bind* are social: comprised of subjects,
bodies, and discourses. Prior to any photography, *Double Bind*'s
enactment commenced at the moment I initially proposed the
project to my ex-wife, Meghan Ledare-Fedderly. Articulating

something that couldn't be taken back, my invitation set real confrontations, events, and risks into play. Meanings took shape in relation to the individual desires, and intersubjective disclosures and nondisclosures, of *Double Bind*'s three participants—in this case *intimates*, cast in a triangle as husband, (ex-)wife, and ex-husband. While the transpiring conversations, concessions, and push/pull amongst the participants exceeded the limits of the photographic indexical, *Double Bind* recast representation as interrelational, foregrounding a space of speculation circuitously threading through the subjective lenses of its participants. This speculative space functioned for each participant as a space of play and experimentation, a medium to both performatively sound out ourselves and to reconstitute our interrelations anew; we each used *Double Bind*'s structure and constraints for our own personal (and intersubjective) ends.

The social theorist Niklas Luhmann observes that within the autopoiesis, or self-reproduction, of systems, systems constitute their own products. Within this circuit, affect functions as a catalyst, something that can be directed, but which, importantly, resists being fully determined. Affect's multivalent meanings, constantly unfolding, hinge on contingency. Its messages nominate their recipients, who in turn must attune themselves and individuate a position relative to affect's call before they might respond, or add, to its loop of communication. Casting photography as feedback, *Double Bind* asks its subjects to negotiate—and act upon—the restraints and controls of its system in order to map these affective, interrelational dynamics.

As subjects we circulate ourselves as representations and mediate our positions through the visual field. *Double Bind* poses an allegorical relation between individual subjects (including the performative relations between them) and relations which appear as representations within a broad collection of printed mass-media materials (a social field comprised of multiple subjective representations, with all their attendant desires, collective dissimulations, and means of distancing). With this slip in scale— and this slipping between private and public relations, between roles, responsibilities, actions, and reactions—complicity is confused. My role is also slippery: enacting my own position and interrelations, I must also enact the same dynamics that I'm calling into question. Stepping into this double bind constitutes a refusal to play games of dissimulation. It is to subject oneself to the trials and tribulations surrounding the consumption of spectacle.

My dialogue with Rhea Anastas constitutes yet another disordering. This book intends not to limit interpretations of the work, but rather to complicate the process of viewing and reading it. *Double Bind*, the installation and this book, aims to redress spectacle without falling into the sterile critiques of so-called correct positions. Within the dialogue as encounter, Anastas and I reflect on and perform how play is infused throughout *Double Bind*—through humor, pathos, absurdity, trauma, sexuality . . . the whole mess.

Double Bind's excess and scale—the occasionally unmanageable volume of materials and affects within the piece—and the specificities entailed within each of our viewing positions ensured that the most either of us could be were singular subjects, viewers. Differently put, within this dialogue, the two of us are another of the work's dyads: Anastas and I complicate each other's positions, working on each other, just as the piece works on us. Authority and "critical distance" are impossible, just as our thought is not fixed or stable, but rather changeable and wholly contingent. From every point, interpretation begins anew, and the reader, like the viewer, is asked to take up a field of problems.

As both an artwork and as this dialogue, *Double Bind* serves as a mirror. This mirror implicates its viewers in a series of questions. What do I see? What do I *desire* to see? How might *Double Bind* presence what can't be seen? Shifting from the ocular to an ecology and context of meaning-making, what is revealed? Perhaps most crucially: What games, which desires and expectations . . . *what* is it that we want from our engagement with art?

3. Dialogue — Rhea Anastas and Leigh Ledare

I.

LEIGH LEDARE: I want to ask how you experience the work, what happens for you as a viewer? Early on in our conversations, you mentioned this affective or emotionally charged, but ambiguous, quality you find in *Double Bind*. How does that operate?

RHEA ANASTAS: My first response, and it's one that continues, is that I feel divided by the work. I'm aware of the fact that I'm able to intellectualize my experience, and doing so involves following the material structures of the work, and its conceptual and political involvements. But there's more to it than that.

For the photographing of *Double Bind*, you organized two trips to a rental cabin in upstate New York, somewhere you had never before been. You spent three days there with Meghan Ledare-Fedderly, your ex-wife, and afterward Meghan and her new husband, Adam Fedderly, took the same trip for the same number of days, staying in the same cabin. Meghan and Adam's participation had been worked out in advance: *Double Bind* began with an invitation, which they accepted. The two stays are scripted from the relationships described above, so there's an element of working autobiographically and an element of composing, of putting this relationship triangle into play, enacting it; so there's at the same time amplification or artifice that's involved. The photographs that were produced during each trip comprise the public portion of *Double Bind*, its documentation. The two sets of approximately five hundred photographs each are kept distinct and color-coded. I can see your decisions about format, using 35 mm and shooting in black and white, as well as the consistency of using every single frame on the film rolls from the trips and hand-developing, in this unedited form.

The work's nearly one thousand black-and-white photographs are presented in two distinct ways. They are presented in stacks within two vitrines, and a number of them are also displayed within the work's wall-hung panels. You also incorporate a collection of print-media artifacts into the piece. This includes many images which were photographically generated and then distributed through the popular press. Although entirely external to the shooting I just described, within a large group of the panels some of this imagery is combined with additional photographs taken during the two trips. Additionally, print-media materials are presented alone within the work's third vitrine. Something like six thousand torn pages (and some intact periodicals) are gathered within this case in a dense massing of piles, with parts and pages of the piles covering other parts.

And, I should say, you generated a multivolume publication around the time of the Los Angeles exhibition of *Double Bind: Husbands, Diptychs*, and *Ephemera*.

It takes time to isolate and speak about the visual and cognitive relationships, disjunctions, and so on that come across within the elements of this multifaceted work. Each element is also intense in its own right.

> When I'm asked to discuss *Double Bind* I typically find myself highlighting its structure as a complex system. My impulse isn't to overcorrect potential misreadings, but rather to point to how *Double Bind* uses structure to situate its subjects, ordering their relations and the controls present between them, in a way that informs the internal complexity of the piece. I also emphasize this to distinguish how I think *Double Bind* differs from normal practices of photographing the personal and its affects.

> These structural decisions are introduced and framed by a text I wrote, which hangs on the wall as part of the installed work. The text serves both as a script for the participants' performances, including my own, and also as an introduction for the viewer. It announces and links the work's two comparative structures: the intersubjective dynamics of *Double Bind*'s two trips, the use of the camera as a feedback mechanism to record Meghan within each situation; and a second comparative structure, the paralleling of these private images with public images from the collection of printed mass-media materials.

I see *Double Bind*'s complex structure before me, but to reason this way would be to say nothing about what happens to me when I view the work, what kinds of thoughts and feelings it evokes. These well up before, during, and within the activity of theorizing that I am also doing as I view, and they complicate that theorizing.

> And that felt dimension, which runs counter to an indexical reading of photographic representation, is of course a crucial part of the work. While indexical readings present themselves concretely, the work elicits an emotional response. That response, which is much more difficult to pinpoint, is made manifest in the relations between people.

This is one of the tensions I want to locate within the piece: my experience erupts and breaks off from any single interpretive mechanism I might use. I can't help having this bodily reaction to *Double Bind*. It has to do with contact, more than emotions as such—with affect. I'm inside the work, within its projective space, and without knowing it I am made alert to looking and being looked at—to seeing Meghan's face and body, over and over again. I am caught up in looking, and I am riven, finding myself doing my own looking, and yet also very turned off by it, engulfed in moments of not liking it. This is what is entailed in witnessing these acts of looking at Meghan, and adding my own acts to those that were performed. I can start to speak as a feminist about disidentifying more than identifying with these relations of looking.

> Well, that emotional response is one layer of what we might think of as an excess in *Double Bind*. But I'd also suggest that there's another register that the situation's construction and this comparative mode put into play. Even if the primary, personal aspect of the work centers on representations of Meghan, the viewer still has to hold the details of these multiple relationships in her head simultaneously, and minding those gaps materializes intersubjective dynamics that are conspicuously absent, that can't be captured as photographic information. Through mapping a constellation of relations, those obviated spaces are made apparent, opening onto the pathways of each participant's agency.

I mean, the photos of Meghan show us what, to try to be more precise? The black and whites are traces based in the appearance and expression of the female body, and they are loaded: woman as image, Meghan as icon, a woman as photographed by two men. The archetype has a specificity, passing from a marriage that's ended to another marriage—it also has a repetition, the mirroring of one couple by another. And you're not just staging this situation once but twice, as though you're putting the problem in bold *and* underlining it.

I do believe that affect, or agency, won't be represented if it's mostly described in structural terms—that is, those of received feminist and theoretical critiques. *Double Bind* lays out a specific picturing of subjectivities that emphasizes the intersubjective. Is it feedback rather than structure? Can we say the images are staged in this way?

The objects and subjects of desire and love (mutually identifying, attracting, as well as splitting or differentiating) are made present in an active way. This needs to be argued more thoroughly: Why, or how? This gets us to the layer that may depart from the layer of sexual difference. I wonder, too, if these experiences and relations are, to a great extent, unseen?

> Frequently photography locates the female figure as muse, a role that is both elevated and deprecating—and it seems to me that these images enact a lot of that same contradictory movement. *Double Bind* situates the viewer within this ambivalent space, stuck between identifying with the tropes of romantic sentiment and expressivity, even obsession, and the structural critiques the piece opens up. It nests these irreconcilable viewpoints inside each other, so that the viewer is caught vacillating between them—is that partly what you come away with?

Partly, but even after coming to terms with my first response, this complexity keeps prodding me. It prompts me to question more deeply what *Double Bind* actually presents—not only what can be seen, but also what it presents to be known about what is seen, and how. To undo or let go of feminist tools for a moment, what else surrounds the imagery? If we let the linguistic analysis of sexuality, through sexual difference and other symbolizations, reify and fix the whole range of interpretive and experiential possibilities, we risk losing access to all the contingencies of participating in the work.

> *Double Bind*'s temporal staging and feedback also suggest something about our private interiority—by that I mean not only my own, but also that of the other participants. These dynamics play out through the narrative situation and through the sequence of its staging, which unfold as a set of stimulations and responses. And any response at any given moment is inevitably influenced by concerns which are psychically present to certain participants, but nonetheless can't be seen: that absent presence described by André Green's psychoanalytic notion of the third.

I'm aware that I'm receiving the imagery from a position that is necessarily external to its having been produced, but that also remains a very implicated or implicating position.

> Maybe that lies in how *Double Bind* confronts the viewer with this profusion of imagery and positions. While it stages spectatorship, it situates this act inside a structure that presents a very specific angle onto these materials, and one that might not necessarily be comfortable for the viewer.

Well, perhaps angles, as in multiple, not only one angle. Broadly speaking, there are two image types in *Double Bind*: those of Meghan seen from the two shooting events, alongside the proliferation of other imagery found in the mass-media images you've collected. This media material includes "lifestyle" images depicting couples and relationships; hetero- and homoerotic photography, be it in the form of advertising or editorials or pornography; advertisements for services and luxury goods; and pages drawn from cultural sections, or sections that report on history or travel. In smaller doses, this aggregation of materials also reflects political reporting, in pages about social and racial issues in the US, or in articles drawn from the height of Cold War interactions between the US and Russia. Let's assume that these different orders of imagery communicate in distinct ways, and that we can't simply overlook this.

I think we do need recourse to traditional feminist tools to be critical toward the social dynamics and agencies that may be foreclosed by the gendered scripting of culture, a foreclosure reflected both in the media imagery and in the many photographs shot during the trips.

It's difficult to view *Double Bind* in any kind of stable way on the scale of presentation that the work uses and at the level of detail— or is it accumulation?—that it presents. I literally can't take it in, and in moments, as I watch myself regarding this sexual-difference narrative, a narrative for me about contemporary theory itself, I almost can't stand it.[1]

> And I'd argue that this is the point! *Double Bind* centers its subjects and the viewer on its representations in order to foreground these asymmetries that we might not want to recognize, so as to stress that we're not over these issues—we're not in a postgender situation, for one. This extends to suggest how as singular subjects we're submitted, and submit ourselves, to systems; how we're written by discourse, how we trade on our autonomy, with all the trappings that accompany this.

Yes, but what I really want to emphasize is how caught up I am in viewing, in the fundamental raw vocabularies and affects of the sets of performed and found images, and to express how weighted and full of variable feeling and response this space is for me.

> You mean because viewing art can risk becoming overintellectualized? And pieces like *Double Bind* present us with all this irreconcilability, these visceral contradictions that exceed what can be cleanly rationalized?

I mean the limits to what is reasoned-through within an analytical viewpoint—the ordering and the sense of, well, control, that generates. It has its artificial side, that reliance on order and analytical distance.

Don't the mass-media stereotypes that *Double Bind* makes central have to do with gender and culture, and what seeing means within the models of feminist and other critiques that we have about looking and the subject? It has occurred to me that *Double Bind* may give such a primary position to this imagery of sexual difference for the complex reason of bringing us into a more heterogeneous space of social dynamics, intimacy, sexuality.

> Is this to say that *Double Bind* complicates those feminist theories of the gaze, or mass culture's strategies of containment and scripting of positions—possibly to ask how we use them, or have used them, and what their effects are? I think we have to look at how subjects are shaped through these discursive systems, which in turn might present their own confinements. But rather than attributing good or bad values to these things, I'd suggest that what culture presents us with are limits to be negotiated . . .

My identification, or disidentification, yours, others'—each viewing needs to be stressed as an active process.

> It's important to note that we're using our actual roles as husband, (ex-)wife, and ex-husband within the staging of the work. Submitting ourselves to *Double Bind*'s structure, and taking up its proximity to autobiography, allows each of us to stage a doubled, reflective relationship to our actual roles. It plays with that gap in order to twist the effects of participating and viewing. On the other hand, *Double Bind* can't escape being read in line with its use of literal relations—it insists on that, which surfaces things often excluded by way of the theoretical: sex, but also intimacy, shame, frustration, confusion, and any number of other intensities interwoven with identification. There's a risk that comes with presenting this—a strong possibility that the viewer, even unconsciously, will implement certain defense mechanisms so as not to encounter this complexity that the work mirrors back to them.

To view from a defensive stance is complicated. What if the viewer is not forthright about it?

Right, there are these limits. And negotiating these gaps may continue, or may cease at a certain point. The viewer's process of navigating depends on personal beliefs and experiences. But those reactions are also important; those responses frame another facet of the work's meaning, an underside, and a lot of questions crop up from where the work may test or trigger existing conflicts and beliefs.

One of the foundations of feminist dissent toward patriarchal norms has been to reposition praxis as central, and by that I mean the kinds of understandings that are gained experientially. Though these can never exist or be known outside the social and cultural, these experiences are something I want to be inclusive toward—I want to comprehend them as structurally key to both challenging and forming the descriptive and the theoretical.

Well, there's the position that I occupy simply by virtue of my being a specific historical subject, and that comes with a certain baggage. But in my case—as with, in turn, yours, and other viewers', whoever they might be—subjectivity is never reducible to an essentialized position alone. It's important to qualify this. Myself, I identify with the position of an informed male viewer who is knowing about and sensitive toward the social asymmetries taken up by feminist critiques. In the work, however, I'm also attempting to inhabit my contradictions, and—through presenting multiple positions in relation to my own—to position the viewer between both sides of the problem, straddling all those conflicting spaces for identification and its cancellation. It puts that irreconcilability onto the viewer, who is then caught trying to find certainty inside a situation where there is none, where it's destabilized.

That feminist critique, seen from your viewing position, well, it's not a certainty for me by any means as I view the piece. For one, there is the vast array of beliefs and viewpoints of the media collection. The viewer's position is greatly affected by this, I don't know what to call it, slipping, shifting, openness, permissiveness . . . It's the opposite of art that directs the viewer from a superior position, from outside as it were.

But that outside might still find its way inside the piece, in that the viewer carries it with them into the gallery. Another way to say this is that while the viewer has a job to work on the piece, the piece also works on them. In that sense, the meaning of the piece can't be predigested—it's contingent and continues to unfold. Maybe this is what you point to by that experience of feeling yourself divided. There's a tendency to pathologize what we might be able to locate as the cause of this kind of instability. At the same time, this functions as a catalyst, and *Double Bind* nominates the viewer to individuate their own values and viewpoints against the contradictions and conflicts it stages.

I also have a need here to examine my relationship to a detached, critical mode of analysis. I came to *Double Bind* through the burden of the set of relationships and identifications that were figured within the production and perception of my past bodies of work, especially *Pretend You're Actually Alive*.² If we take subjects, bodies, and discourses to be the actual materials of an artwork, then I also have to account for my own subjective historical position. Certain personal dynamics were and remain semi-inescapable, in the sense that life throws each of us into a given set of circumstances. The question is, where am I in that imagery? How am I inhabiting the images within the structure of the work: not as a self-expression, but in order to make visible a set of issues, to question the dynamics and positions that come along with them? How does the subjective speak more broadly to cultural conditions? Is fatigue—as a condition of masculinity or patriarchy, or even their critical counterpositions—exposed? Are the flaws within white-male privilege, and more broadly authority, revealed? How do I perform and stage the performance of these conditions? In other words, how am I exhibiting self-criticism toward my own role in my work, but also complicating roles or definitions possibly projected onto me from those receiving the work? Approaching *Double Bind* in this way, I'm attempting to tap into these affects and emotions that underwrite our shared social landscape: codes that are deeply internalized and that at the same time we may not want to acknowledge.

Well, we seem to need to remind ourselves over and over again in the political space of feminism that men *and* women can identify with masculine positions that have been historically occupied only by men, and that anyone is able to disidentify with those positions (or not), or may identify with feminist challenges to those positions.

We experience *Double Bind* as being narrated and performed on one level through the heteronormative rubric of marriage and the expectations associated with woman-as-icon images. So I am talking about the orders and genderings of that voyeuristic space and the discourse associated with its objectifications since Laura Mulvey, Victor Burgin, and others; and since Adrian Piper, who theorized whiteness and blackness within the controls and orders of the aesthetic. But on another level, we experience the complicated, fragmentary view of intimate situations that the shooting events perform and put on display.

Double Bind's depictions of loaded scenes of voyeurism may anticipate feminist and other structural critiques, solicit them even. But is this a closed loop? Or is it an opening onto another story, one that offers all of this in such a way that we also may identify, and see things otherwise? Is that how the complicity can operate, and the promising reorientation of analytical models that we've been describing?

1. Our description of the media material follows one that appears in an interview between Ledare and David Joselit. In this interview, which was conducted for an exhibition catalogue, Joselit brought a new degree of theoretical scrutiny to *Double Bind*. See "David Joselit and Leigh Ledare: *An Interview*," in *Leigh Ledare, et. al.*, ed. Elena Filipovic (Brussels: WIELS Contemporary Art Centre; Milan: Mousse Publishing, 2012), 91–133.

2. *Pretend You're Actually Alive*, a photographic work Ledare developed between 2001–2008, which was exhibited for the first time, and published as a book, in 2008. Ledare produced this project's photographs collaboratively with Tina Peterson, the central subject or protagonist of the series and Ledare's mother. Trained in ballet, Peterson was successful as a dancer before raising Ledare and his brother in Seattle, WA. In *Pretend You're Actually Alive*, color photographs of Peterson, as well as images Ledare took of other family members, are grouped with assorted ephemera, including documents, photographs from family albums, and notes written in the first person. Peterson's self-presentation is forthright in its sexual display, and Ledare pinpoints this genre of photography (which has precedents, such as Larry Clark's *Tulsa*) as she poses deliberately and expressively, according to her own self-stylizations in collaboration with Ledare, wearing lingerie, full makeup, and other adornments. In a handful of rolls, Peterson performs sexual acts, autoerotically and with partners.

II

LEIGH LEDARE : Maybe we can start by looking at two of the framed photographs from the small group that exist as single photographs, enlarged slightly and spread throughout the installation.

RHEA ANASTAS : The photographs within *Double Bind* are coded according to the two shooting events of your first trip with Meghan, followed by Adam's, and are presented, respectively, on either black or white backgrounds—a color code that serves to index the images as either yours or his. So one structure is that through diptychs, the two couple's sets of images are ordered against each other. But the two photographs you are speaking of are from a smaller group of ten photographs that are simply framed full bleed, distinct from the other works, right?

Correct, and presenting these photographs "straight," as a counterpoint to *Double Bind*'s comparative structure, stresses the typical way photographs are read—that is, indexically. This was a kind of reminder about the limitations of reading images exclusively through a representational lens, according to assumptions about the thing indexed in the photograph.

In the first example—a photograph that I made of Meghan—what can be seen is her lying atop a white duvet. The bed has been freshly made. Above a cropped sliver of waistline (falling mostly outside the image's lower left corner), her bare upper body is visible. She leans back onto one elbow and rotates slightly toward the camera. In the center of the image, her dark hair, which is pulled behind her and fastened into a bun, frames her face in semiprofile. Her right hand reaches across her chest, clasping her other wrist. The effect is drawn sharply: this causes the shoulder closest to me to raise and roll slightly inward—framing her breasts, and simultaneously framing her breasts out. What she presents for the camera actually amounts to an active refusal to present herself.

I think where Meghan is looking is important. With eyes turned, she returns your look and the viewer's.

And her look is confrontational—her withdrawal juts forward, it cancels. The single image also allows us to deconstruct that reciprocity around the looks, those both inside and outside the frame, as well as the possible voyeurism active in viewing. This image doesn't read merely as a document of something that's happened, but knowing the narrative of the trips complicates this even further. You have to see it as one link in an unfolding chain of communication, a kind of tactical event, one enacted for me and for the camera—and the intensity of how her self-objectification is directed extends that performance. Projecting her apparent ambivalence with these roles and expectations around being looked at, Meghan negates the looks directed at her—at once my look, but also the viewer's. This manufactures a skewed space for my own identification in relation to Meghan, not to mention for the viewer's.

But couldn't the same look be a dissembling for Adam's benefit? I could think of the image as reflecting what the comparison may set up as a condition of competition between two men.

Yeah, but this is where the viewer has to sort through whether the familiar is the familiar or the familiar made strange, or something else . . . The viewer has to sort that out from where they're positioned in a doubled way: made to identify through the exchange of looks within the photographs; and, through the mapping function of the piece, made to be outside the situation witnessing these relations.

There are multiple acts of looking crossing each other, implicating each of you, and the viewer as well, in a reciprocal field of relations: her active role as performer, your and Adam's roles as photographers photographing her, and (through an address distilled within and projecting out from inside the photograph) our roles as viewers viewing.

You might well be modeling the viewer's viewing in *Double Bind*. Meghan might have another response to the situation, another mood and her own ideas about returning your look, Adam's look, and the public's look. The evidence could be read as a performance of appealing modesty.

I agree with you—if by that you mean that modeling the viewer's understanding consists of staging situations that first elicit default expectations, as a prerequisite for then complicating those expectations. I do see the viewer's viewing as something malleable, a material that can be modeled—but that process is not unidirectional. Her viewing is also something that she must individuate and model in response. It's intersubjective—and I have to respond to viewers' responses in turn.

But let's come back to the single photographs for one moment . . . How do the images in this situation of exchange foreground the importance of the act of reading, and the viewer's and participants' exchanges, in the work? What happens in Adam's photographs?

Okay, take this image here, an image Adam made of Meghan. Apart from a nightshirt and a pair of knee-high black socks, Meghan is nude. She is lying on one side of the same bed that's seen in my photograph. Her hair is down. Her head rests against her open forearm. On the bedside table a hair clip and two bobby pins sit beside a clock. The same duvet is in this instance pushed down to one corner of the bed. On the pillow beside her can be discerned the impression of the photographer's head, but he's now positioned behind the camera. Meghan's eyes can be observed concentrating on a book—a travel guide standard for this type of vacation rental—but her ass, bare and viewed in posterior, directly confronts us. Framed by her open legs and bent knee, her crotch constitutes a bull's-eye within the image, centering a reflection on (or an anticipation of) a sexual intercourse that her and the photographer have either recently completed or soon will, and this is all displayed to me and to the viewer. At the same time, she looks off disinterestedly.

It's kind of a trophy picture.

Well, it's definitely one of the more erotically pointed images from Adam and Meghan's trip, and from the nearly one thousand total images of Meghan attributed to either Adam or myself. That said, we have to be careful not to reduce the character of either of our image sets exclusively to the above two examples. I could just as easily point out an image of Adam's where Meghan is dressed elegantly in an overcoat and high socks, standing in dappled light on a small leaf-covered lane; or another image of his, where she's clothed and smiling gently, drenched in this beautiful window light.

Yes, there are dozens of tones, genres, and looks within his nearly five hundred photos, and there's a broad range within yours as well. That said, I think these physically overt, loaded moments comprise a structure in their own right, and in viewing I think I initially focus very much on this erotic horizon to orient where I stand in relation to the work. Their charge is highly pitched, it bleeds or overruns onto all of the images, imprinting my responses to the images that show other forms of intimacy, other poses.

It's true—attention is drawn first to these sexualized components. That, and also how the system submits the subject to a set of controls, which is important for the reason that it reflects how these structures drown out more subtle forms of intimacy and agency that are also present.

When you mention control, I think of a parallel to Gregory Bateson's ideas and his emphasis on the conserving aspect of the individual's psychology. "Self–corrective" is Bateson's term for the systemic condition. In Bateson's view, the subject learns to maintain the status quo within a social system or environment.

There is the representation—what it captures, the expectations of reading—and there are the position-based responses that happen for viewers. But none of these can be read as isolated. Each image of Meghan has to be read as the result of either one or the other of the two relationships, in each case two people articulating something to the missing third, and each step in the process constituting a link in a chain of feedback whose active back and forth emerges as, and shapes, discourse. Meaning isn't fixed—neither for the participants inside the piece, nor for the viewer, who is also offered multiple positions to identify from.

Understanding one's relation to the piece takes work. Meaning is contingent and unfolds in stages.

In that sense, *Double Bind* is a system on multiple levels, and discursively too. The viewer is directed into the experience one way, but the initial cues for reading the piece shift and the meaning *détourns*. *Double Bind* attempts to reproblematize the scene we're left with following the mass-cultural recuperation of these types of transgressive images.

Would that put readings that may fix these lived identifications, reducing them to a structural interaction between photographer/ subject, or man/woman, or other viewpoints which might be naïve to these structural issues, in the realm of the unreliable?

I am thinking about what you've observed. I don't see it as a relativism, one that would level the multiple meanings and positions to be equivalents. You, Meghan, Adam: each of you have distinct positions through the narrative, but there's also your privileged position as the one organizing this structure.

I also want to point out that as a viewer I have the feeling that something is being projected onto me. Or that I'm being pushed around by the piece, pressured up against the norms or Bateson-like conserving of the system.

In a similar way to how culture functions, a work such as *Double Bind* has to manufacture means to implicate the viewer, centering her on certain readings and responses, producing or anticipating the viewer's reactions to the piece. It inhabits the system to produce feedback that then comes to inform it, but it's a way of harnessing this toward a mode of questioning. This discursive set up, at least aspects of it, parallels the scripting of psychosocial observations within *Double Bind*'s initial performances. The address of the work coerces the viewer into a situation that draws something out of her. It hails her.

This may also throw into relief ways that reception might be prefigured by discourse, how we're made subject to discourse, and made to reproduce its values, or even to pay lip service to it—this, despite how our experience might open onto more nuanced understandings of the complexities of a situation.

A lot of this hinges on the erotic in, or as, projection. And a measure of complicity is unavoidable for the viewer. This is one of the sources of the viewer's discomfort or pleasure or something in between.

But this is not for no reason; it's not merely the incendiary and its affects that I'm after. I think I am trying to get at a paradox: that *Double Bind* has to rely on projection as the vehicle through which it can open onto these issues of social self-regulation, internalization, expression, and convention or norm. Having done that, having turned the participants and viewers toward those dynamics, however, they're actually made to think about them as opposed to simply turn away. I want the viewer to be implicated, rather than rest in a distanced location, with the default act of refusal that ultimately leaves recourse only to projection, simplification, and so on. This push and pull is key.

At the same time, there is this functioning of the intimate as an address.

As a technique in the work? Or as a solicitation, a drawing-into this realm of experience? Here is where the work's most private qualities, what feels like an insistence upon interiority, come into focus.

Double Bind invites the viewer in, and yet it also mirrors their intrusion back to them. Perhaps this is one of the ways *Double Bind* deals with the autobiographical expectations that followed *Pretend*.

The private that becomes public through the viewer. It's a dynamic, I should say, partly . . . But, you've raised the comparison with *Pretend*, and here there is a difference, it seems to me, around the way an understanding of culture and the social as a system becomes a language or vocabulary of the work. I get the feeling that with *Double Bind*, this next time around with the work that's following *Pretend*, you're hyperconscious of imposing a structure: the relationship triangle, two husbands, two trips . . .

> Sure. There's also a set of presumptions put in place through a kind of quasi-scientific set of controls and a scripting of experience: two couples undergoing the same experiences, same number of days, same number of rolls of film, as if this degree of objectivity could actually reveal something, some factual data we could see.

It's almost as if there's a reference to scientific processes of gathering information, the camera being cast as detached, as technical and recording—you've already referred to it as a feedback mechanism— which in sight of the subjective conditions carries a degree of absurdity, something which I actually find quite hilarious.

> The humor of the work is something we can talk more about, but your comment also brings to mind performances of the early seventies, such as Dan Graham's *Two Consciousness Projection(s)* or *Past Future Split Attention*.

Okay, but from the first mention of the triangle, there immediately arises a sexual expectation. It brings to mind the fraught interpersonal terrain of the "love triangle," which classically carries a set of very loaded connotations. But rather than being incendiary, I read this erotic address as an attempt to draw out an affective structure that places the viewer into a different situation, calling the viewer forth through its charged space. If you respond to the sexual opening, you follow it—whether it opens up a space you're taking pleasure in or being critical of, or both. I could say there is anticipation and also dissonance, or better, worry around limits and control, or self-control. This in turn could solicit moral or shame-based readings, but being implicated also makes me understand that I'm not in the purview of analytic distance. The voyeuristic relation is also opened, shifted—you and Adam, well, we can't say that you have a purely voyeuristic

relationship to the situations, because of being implicated within
your respective relationships with Meghan and each other. Instead,
it's identificatory.

> What's atypical about *Double Bind*'s invitation to look is that
> one interpretation is forced to rub up against another, mirroring
> back to the viewer expectations she might be bringing to viewing.
> My hope was to create a system of meanings that echoed this
> irreconcilability in the visual field, but showed also how it was
> being put into play. There are certain liberties the piece takes in
> relation to directing, or even manipulating the viewer, as a means
> to activate that space so the complexity of these issues can continue
> to unfold. This is counter to how anxiety may create an impulse
> for composure.

> I think from the viewer's perspective, we have to ask: What
> response does it create, what does it put in motion, this doubled
> shooting scenario that so intentionally tempts an interpretation of
> rivalry? Is there also a discursive side to this rivalry?

Well, first off, the rivalry has a narrative role, isn't that unmistakably
the case?

> Still, we should be very careful not to assume that this comparative
> structure is one that's simply competitive.

I need you to speak more about that. I feel like you are offering
rivalry as a device of the work, and then now sort of diminishing
its uses.

> I'll try to clarify how this functions as a tool. *Double Bind* does
> stage a dynamic that's open to being interpreted as rivalry, but it's
> slippery—I'm staging this rivalry precisely to tempt this reading,
> while at the same time attempting to challenge it as a false binary.

> We need to question whether or not this perceived rivalry is a
> projection. By this I don't necessarily mean the viewer's, but rather
> one that the viewer perceives I'm placing on them by situating

them within the charged space of this imagery. The situation triggers and draws to the surface some kind of deep-seated defense mechanism, one perhaps fixated on, and in turn taking up, binary thinking: either/or, win/lose, have/have-not, etc.

Whether it's to possess something, or to establish hierarchies around gender, class, or race, or to insist on the authority of a singular discourse, what's that impulse to take satisfaction and attempt to make it conclusive, to frame it as a thing, as though it were akin to private property, something that through authority someone could own or keep? I think we anticipate satisfaction as being linked to these more egotistical motives of competition or revenge.

The tradition of visual language to which the shooting events refer involves an asymmetrical, colonizing relation to a woman's body, and sexual and visual access to it, typing the body for or according to that access.

Of course. I can't rule out that certain aspects of Meghan's objectification might be tied up with this. But I want to challenge the assumption that the comparative premise behind *Double Bind* is merely functionalizing, or that it ends strategically at any sort of clear-cut, stable resolution. In my mind, *Double Bind* isn't about conclusiveness. Rather than competition, I'd argue that it's much more about staging contradiction, which is where it stems from: using oneself to question, toward an experimental end.

I'm curious about how this contradiction plays out, how it might say something about our overdetermination of the credulity of others or ourselves. This attempt for certainty in meaning might be read as an intimation of wished-for satisfaction, drawing toward some conclusion we perceive as necessary in moving forward, and necessary to categorization. Each participant has their own narrative angle through which they enter the work—rivalry perhaps, though from another position some other story might be more plausible, some other way of counteracting the uncertainty and complexity of *Double Bind*'s contradictory intentions and emotions.

This is an exchange, then, about describing an undermining of inherited meanings in *Double Bind*. How is this distinct from a withholding of meaning-making?

> There's also something about me starting from a position of apparent failure that is crucial, my position of having been written out of marital relations with Meghan, of occupying the space of this trip from an outside—the inside now being her and Adam's marriage. The authorship structure of the piece, networked and containing the traces of each subject's agency, but ultimately organized under my name, in turn comes to complicate this. It's a counterstaging, an expropriation of value, another loaded condition of the work that the viewer has to have an opinion toward.

I could follow a logic that would cast your lack in a different light. A fairly paranoid-type response on the part of Meghan and Adam to your overture to photograph alone with her could take the form of something like, "anything the two of you may do, we can do more extremely; we have thought of all of this." Your invitation could be the cause, the effect being the display of sexual ownership in their performances. Such paranoid logic aside, your position of failure/lack could create such responses.

> Sure, and that content may hail the subject. Those positions may be something the structure conjures, and this is tied to how the structure reproduces itself through subjects, and that really interests me! The performance of subjective relations in *Double Bind*, which takes place in a photographic present but opens onto the space of the three participants' pasts, presents, and futures, creates an allegory, where the complexity of this triangle has to be read back onto how containment structures have functioned inside the appropriated historical past of the media images, with all the lessons we know from this.

Really, how is sexuality used in the work? What effects does it have on expectations, on viewing?

Contrary to seeing sexuality as an expression of desire, or regarding it simply from the perspective of how it's used to hail us, I want to reveal how it might be made to function as a means of attending to the anxiety of position, scripting various hierarchical relations. *Double Bind* tries to get at these questions. How could I be delivering something through one ideological vehicle that *détourns* into something else?

Knowing what we know through the script's narrative, Adam's images might be made out of reaction to the ambiguity of my position; as a response to where I perhaps shouldn't be, or to possible desires that Meghan and I might still hold for one another, or other intentions I might have. This plays off anxieties around what can't be seen, and this may be folded into Adam and Meghan's response. It's interesting what Adam's images may say about ownership, desire, and its representation—nesting an invitation to look inside a contradictory articulation of possession, which in turn defines my own apparent position of lack.

This may also define the visual limitations of how Meghan might appear within this scenario. But do those limitations speak to her agency, or is this simply how they appear to the viewer's perception, in the narrowed context of what is visible? Again, that limited bandwidth of the photographic image is foregrounded, but *Double Bind* constellates these representations, which points to how that interrelational space constitutes an economy, one that underwrites the image.

It is important to acknowledge that aspect. At the same time, I can't say conclusively that Adam's role is fixed in that way for me as I view the entirety of his images. On the other hand, even if I were to reduce each of your images to probing and flirtation, your advance as the respectful one may be no less sexually driven, just differently approached.

Or, let's guess at another possibility, that your images speak back to Adam and Meghan's routinized, sexualized ones. If their sex is in some respects pictured as a trophy to show you, your response goes after something distinct, other registers. Is your concealing of Meghan, with Meghan, protective? Is it feminist, a more progressive image? I actually find that to be a weak theory, a weak moral logic.

> Well, with your qualification of it being a more progressive image aside, this could be a completely plausible reading. But also, let's not forget that appearances can be deceptive, that they can be manipulated and made to conceal, or made to appear moral.

And I actually don't want to reduce the performances of the work and the multiple exchanges to the register of visibility, for one, or to surface, or to heteronormative readings of sexual expression. Because much of what happens and passes between the couples is beneath the image and language, inchoate, unknowable and utterly private.

But inverting that reasoning that I can do, directing myself out of explaining what may lie on the visual register, I still have to think through seeing Meghan photographed over and over again. How do the intimate images between the three of you read as types? This is really fascinating and fraught. It leads to readings like the ones I just played out. They are biased, subjective, moral, sentimental, and so on.

Why is this structure of doubling, its complicity with stereotypes and its response of "good and bad" types, so crucial, this comparative structure that the project puts into play?

> As a container to hold contradictions, *Double Bind*'s comparative structure maps these images, and others taken by us, both similar and dissimilar, against each other. Ultimately this points to the gaps between representations, and between understandings. Positioned firmly inside a set of subjective relations, *Double Bind* acknowledges that no position is exempt from being complicit. This opens onto a set of questions about subjective judgment, which points to all judgment as being subjective, as being open to bad judgment.

Double Bind's triangulated relationships cast photography's function as multiple: as a catalyst for the performance of self-expression; as communicating and reproducing through individual subjects an existing symbolic system; and finally as a feedback mechanism that might allow us a vantage from which to observe our involvement within the interrelation of these functions.

There is something machine-like about the routinization of the social and cultural that comes forward. The scale may be evidence of photography being cast or allegorized in some sense. But it's complicated to take in. I think we view with expectations: about Meghan's posing, about having been told that you and Adam are in possession of the author function.

And perhaps this is triggered by how *Double Bind*'s authorship structure appears to echo and be aligned with the traditional gender roles on display in the media collection. Opposed to that, however, it has a much more complex, distributed model of authorship. Even though I alone conceived the outline of the performances—and once the two trips were finished, I also arranged the resulting materials into montages and put in place the elements of the comparative structure—each participant also carries an authorship role, one which is tactical; and the degree to which authorship is in flux, contingent and shifting relative to how each of the other participants acts, plays out inside this system. In that sense it was an open system, within which Adam and Meghan could also choose the directions toward which they would take their participation, and through which we all traced out the discrepancies between the positions. One has to notice that the appropriated media materials are woven through with these other strands of individual and cultural authorship too.

There is still this question arising around the management of relations within a differentiated systemic structure such as this. It points to that dialectic between authorship and ownership, which, contextually contingent, we can't simply assume are the same, not in terms of appropriation or observation. One of the more radical things it does is that through the local it shifts the scope of observation to perform as a model of something much larger.

I can see how you self-objectify through taking up authorship, you're embodying it and materializing it, but it's also a very difficult space to self-reflexively occupy. I don't think a certain hierarchy of authorship has dissolved completely in the work, which, after all, is presented under your name, and there are all the forms of your thinking and labor. The distributed aspect of authorship may surround the status of the imagery within the piece. The black and whites and the media collection communicate in a multivocal way. Yes, Meghan and Adam are participants. The viewer is roped in, I have no doubt about that. But there's still a way in which you're the metalevel architect, the one supplying the vision and structure.

> I occupy multiple positions—and yes, one is that of the architect of this piece as a system, which does typically boil down to designating ownership, despite the fact that *Double Bind* duplicates structures that already exist. Pointedly, the work's various functions of authorship and agency are cast as asymmetrical, but this is meant to emphasize these existing, uneven conditions of production. Importantly, there's no concealment of those asymmetries: they're bracketed and manifested to be placed under scrutiny.

> These asymmetries are staged to emphasize a specific detachment— one that may grate for the reason that it has to do with my actively creating a situation only to become the observer. But observing isn't passive, and what *Double Bind* does is it mirrors back to the viewer a structure of complicity that we might choose to see ourselves as exempt from. From there it's our job to consider where we fit into these structures and how we reproduce these systems.

Another implication of regarding the subject in light of this system is, for instance, that there's no essential Meghan, just this functional one, playing a role; but also, importantly, that this role isn't conclusive. This also extends to the two of you as photographers.

Maybe we can look at a diptych, two panels from the group of forty-eight, to telescope our attention from the single images and structure of *Double Bind*, to how meaning is actually being configured through the arrangement of these objects.

Okay, so here, in the first panel of this diptych—a black panel attributed to Meghan and me—you have two photographs. In the first, Meghan stands at the edge of a limestone cliff, positioned between the camera and this drop that overlooks the fog-shrouded lake below. A second image is placed directly underneath this—a landscape that reverses the first viewpoint, which I photographed back from the physical position where Meghan was standing. It shows what Meghan would have seen looking back at me. Only because I'm behind the camera, as the photographer I'm made conspicuously absent, pointing to that visual asymmetry inherent within photographic representation.

You're occupying the spot where she physically stood and you've turned around?

That's right.

On the white panel, two photographs taken by Adam speak to the distinction between the private realm and the public. In an enlarged image, Meghan appears naked on a bed, lying on her side and curled up, fragmented and filling the frame. Overlaid and partially blocking this, a smaller image taken outside at nightfall depicts her fully dressed.

In the image with the bed, as you just said, Meghan is naked with the minor exception of a single tall sock or stocking. We see her underwear in the frame, but the fabric is not covering—the underwear is pulled down and rests lower on her legs.

You're forgetting to say that Adam's erect penis appears in the bottom right of this image's frame—its shape is read against Meghan's sock.

I did glaringly omit that part of the image; I dropped it from my verbalization, anyway. It's embarrassment, I suppose. It's an uncomfortable gesture, as if to say, to exhort, "yeah, look at this."

Meghan is covering her face, and the suggestion is that a sexual act has just occurred. This is the one instance out of nearly five hundred photographs in which Adam includes himself with Meghan, an instance when his body appears within the frame. Perhaps it's how I experienced it, but being that it presents a portrait of his penis, it's hard not to read this as a perverse kind of gift, something aggressively addressed through Meghan to me.

Beyond this, there are multiple images and viewpoints from the print media that are distilled into the panel, such as a clipping that pictures two sides of a single coin, a Ronald Reagan–commemorative dollar with a landscape image on its other side.

The print-media collection is posed as an allegory of the private photographs, within which Meghan also functions problematically as an icon, and this echoes my photographs on the connected black panel. In both cases the photographic transaction is revealed in steps and permutations, through a kind of diagramming of positions.

Partially obscured by the coin is a lushly printed, highly produced pornographic image. What's visible is a teal bedspread on top of which, fragmented, leans a woman's face, her lips parted sensuously—a parallel to what's covered by Meghan's hands in this apparently postcoital image of Adam's. A bowl of blackberries over ice sits beside a drink in a martini glass. It may speak to status, an indicator of consumer and consumed, right? Georges Bataille, also partially obscured, stares down from the upper left corner. At the bottom of this arrangement, a vertical form, a figure or perhaps an effigy, has burst into flames.

How did you choose the pairings? Is that what you did first, before you started intermixing the photographs with the pages from the collection—I mean, did you work with focused comparisons between your photographs and Adam's to begin?

My approach for selecting the images and for ordering each diptych was to propose a reading of those materials and relationships, but one that was speculative. These are fluid responses without any one consistent procedure. I see the diptychs as a series of variations that serve to map the different positions possible around the two sets of relations. There's this layering of possible positions and addresses, which differs from how collages typically construct meaning—here they function more as *montages*, holding different registers against each other, rather than flattening them into one whole. None of these readings are definitive, but rather they're destabilized by the other possible readings presented, each questioning the next, and accruing one after the next.

Counter, then, to the image of Adam's we're talking about, here in this next diptych your black panel contains a grid of eight photographs.

In seven of these photographs Meghan appears within an interior on a bed. This is a stock situation that I asked her to repeat, but there is more to it than that . . .

Meghan seems to be making a lot of choices about how to appear and pose for the camera. She takes her shirt off or doesn't, covers herself. To locate you through the camera, I get the sense that you're being quite changeable, moving around Meghan who is setting up the space through what she is deciding to do, and you're shooting from this. Is it due to Meghan's activity that the images look the way they do?

I'm not so much directing as confronting her with the camera, in a way that creates a heightened dynamic, an acute self-reflexivity. And so much of it is about recording those back-and-forth responses, that cognitive space of being in the situation being photographed, interacting. But again, these gestures can never be fully conclusive. At the same time it's impossible not to read these images and their expressions of intimacy—in distinct ways, both present and blocked—as a result of this relationship and its status relative to Meghan's new marriage.

The looking is conceptualized, made cognitive, due to the wider view and framing which allows us to see how Meghan makes decisions about how to place herself. The heavy, large necklace serves to clothe Meghan, in a manner, along with the fact that she's dressed from the waist down. Conversely, we see her breasts since her upper body is exposed.

> I can also add that the photographs don't fragment Meghan's body. Most of the time they are "medium" shots, shot horizontally, which tends to make clear how Meghan is presenting herself.

Placed on Adam's side of this diptych is a tear sheet from a large-scale advertisement that presents an entire black page surrounded on three sides by a white border, with a tiny caption about a Givenchy dress that isn't pictured.

> This glossy black paper, placed behind the reflective glass from the panel, functions to mirror the viewer back to themselves. There's also a picture of Meghan standing next to a gigantic concrete lawn gnome—and there's humor in that! It might be presumed as another stand-in—for Adam, for me, or even for the viewer who is mirrored back.

Each of the photographs of Meghan has been printed without cropping and is surrounded by a thin white border. You've adhered these directly onto the mat board in each case.

> That border isolates each image as a viewpoint, a frame separating the view from its surrounding context. This becomes especially apparent when multiple images are placed together. Each image, seen as a fragment taken from a larger expanse of time, retains its integrity. This act of framing points to the separate contextual frames present both within the private images and also the public ones.

> Let's look at a very simple panel, which appears on a white background and thus attributes the panel to the relationship between Meghan and Adam. This panel also frames a single tear sheet from a magazine, an advertisement for a bottle of Chivas Regal. A man's hand emerges from a suit jacket to grip the neck

of the bottle, pulling it from a box. We see an untied ribbon and some undone, disheveled tissue paper, no longer standing in the way of the bottle, which resembles an upright phallus. At the bottom of the advertisement, a caption reads: "It's better to give than receive. With certain possible exceptions."

You didn't clip or cut the magazine page—what we see is its actual size?

There was no cropping or cutting. The whole page was torn from an early-seventies lifestyle magazine, and then framed on a white panel. This provokes an intertextual reading. Are the attitudes within the magazines and other images from the collection of ephemera being projected onto the dyad of Meghan and Adam from outside, from me and from the viewer, or are they aligned with expressions originating from Adam and Meghan and projected outward?

The concept of the gift also informed the exchange logic of the various registers of the panels as I worked. Partially, gifting has to do with repressing the terms of exchange, which often pivots around an economy of obligation, expectation, or guilt. I also think of something Derrida said: that what we give when we give gifts is actually time, a temporal space of response. And then there's always Freud's logic of the gift vis-à-vis the anal stage!

Let's talk about another panel that uses the grid, or nearly a grid.

It's almost an itemized list.

I don't feel that it's the logic of typology that this panel puts on view. There are also a lot of references to the human figure, but that's not the organizing principle either. This particular panel appears on black, so it is attributed to you, and it has roughly fourteen fragments, including many color reproductions. The first thing I recognize, positioned as a clipping almost in the center of the panel, is a cheap reproduction torn from a book, a photo of Henri Matisse, who is of course renowned as a colorist, sitting with a model from one of his paintings of odalisques.

Ah yes, and that reproduction, which eliminates color from the scene's lavish textile patterning, reducing it to black and white. It's also framed, like the images of Meghan, by a white border. In terms of recognizable references, there's also an exceptionally stern author photo of Claude Lévi-Strauss from the back of a book jacket and, taken from inside that book, a diagram concerning marriage structures and the exchange of women within patriarchy. Of course the contents of the diagram mirror, in an off way, the triangular structure of the private shooting scenario. It speaks to a structural reading, itself potentially a stereotype, that the scenario may trigger, a reading that in actuality is signaled as having many more layers of complication, given the status of the two marriages and Meghan's actual agency in regards to both relations. There's also a snapshot of my mother . . .

But not one that you took?

No. This is an outtake from another group of photographs that appear in my earlier work with my mother, taken when she was eighteen, standing in front of a set of Doric columns. There's also a sentimental image of an African American woman in a piercing blue sweater, lovingly cradling a tan cat. Then there's a still from Jean Cocteau's *The Blood of a Poet*, where a man appears to be pleading with a woman costumed as a sculpture.

Yeah, a Greek or Roman statue—

She's fragmented and missing her arms. There is a stack of three wedding rings. There's also a fragment with a can of paint that has been capped and is bleeding out the edges. Another fragment depicts a mustached male performer who tips his hat—his head is made up of an inflated balloon, which given a single cartoon eye and mustache might easily be mistaken for a condom. It's phallic. About the performer, I won't hesitate to point out my own mustache, and how a persona is being signaled. What does it all mean?

I also want to differentiate between the innuendo and irony

present in the media, and how I'm choosing to enlist it, how I use a persona to occupy that space, to caricature it. It's a question of how I implicate myself and the stakes of that implication, how it allows me to get under the surface of the situation.

The humor also seems important, or useful, as a counterbalance to the work's identificatory and erotic tensions—and isn't comedy an inevitable part of sex and sexuality, not in the least because of the awkwardness involved in trying to fulfill certain gender scripts/roles that *Double Bind* critiques?

In this panel a few pornographic images also appear. This puts me in that location with the sexualized imagery of Meghan taken by Adam . . .

> Mmm-hmm. And that same space that contains all these different "types" functions as a cultural field, based on representations of intimacy: some pornographic and rather compromised, others artistic or sentimental, and still others that are familial, authorial, apparently biographical, or even anthropological.

Moving onto another panel, this one a diptych, there's a photograph of Meghan with a highly lightened area. She is erased by light. And this heteronormative scene is seemingly changed due to some print-media imagery that's brought into the pair of panels, by the inclusion of vehicles of gay desire.

> Well, Meghan's features are actually blown out by a shaft of light reflecting off her face from a ceiling window. An image of this window also appears within the diptych. This is one of two instances inside the panels in which a private image has not been presented in its entirety, but has been cut in two and separated to span both the white and black sides of the diptych.
>
> One of the private photographs on the white panel, Adam's panel, is flipped and glued face down, concealing Meghan's image and replacing her image with the negative number that I wrote on the back of each photograph as I was printing them. These moments point to what's apparently absent, but also surrounding these representations.

The other features of this collage were taken from a gay porn magazine from the early eighties. The heterosexual norms shift. Two nude male figures are pictured sitting beside each other on a couch, one brown haired and one blond. While this originally constituted one image, it's now been physically bisected and spread across the two panels, each figure suggested as a stand-in for either me or Adam. On the white panel, there is a smaller secondary picture of the two men together. The brown-haired man, first positioned on the panel attributed to me, has crossed over onto Adam's side. He is straddling the other man and, due to the positions, framing, and body language, the act of penetration is evoked.

With the clear division of this panel into "sides" for your photographs and Adam's, there is this satirical or mischievous tone that is emitted—the two husbands; the gay porn models. There are quite a few instances in the framed panels when a male figure—I am thinking too of this image where a man carries a monkey on his back—is presented as clown-like, ridiculous, and so on . . .

That man is ridiculous, but the monkey even more so! The monkey's artist's beret signals him as a stand-in for me, which hints toward self-deprecation. And because of the color of his outfit, the monkey's tan coat blends with the man's tan pants, creating a strange illusion—the monkey's top takes over the man's body. The monkey appears to have this kind of free-wheeling strut, but to see he has to look through the man's head, they're conjoined; whereas the man who carries the monkey on his back appears simply as a torso with sunglasses. The monkey is wielding the man like a camera, the implication being that through recording and transmitting information, the camera in each instance functions as a stand-in for the absent husband.

It's hard to isolate and analyze, but I want to talk about this layering of imagery and identifications, this imagery of male representations and male-male imagery and desire, as locating a position that may not accept the heteronormative binary, that may enframe the marital positions with other cultural and societal roles, casting the normalcy as anything but . . .

That's such an important point. I think of how ideas of the
normative regulate decorum.

I can take these thoughts back to the ones that seem to arise out
of the sexuality performed by Meghan and Adam for the camera.
There are the kinds of pleasures within those acts, and the sensual
and textured, freeing feelings of being nude and sexual, of which
we may be able to see traces. But there are also the framings within
this imagery that I associate with stereotypes and the reduction of
women's bodies to body parts or orifices; that is, split off from the
whole individual and a full exchange of bodies, minds, etc. It's the
contrast between the willing objectifications of two people treating
each other's bodies and erotic zones as objects of desire and use, but
within a full-spectrum relationship, and that directional, arrow-
going-for-target thing about penetration, which is an exercising of
privilege, an isolating of parts.

> To go back, I think there is this trap of falling inside a logic where
> satisfaction is equated with power or credulity, and confusing that
> with actual connection. We might be investing in façades, or
> regulating intimacies through agreed-upon social perceptions.
> In that space of projections we might even find our attachments
> connecting to fantasies rather than actual relations.

> Eve Kosofsky Sedgwick has pointed out that relationships of
> desire which can't be enacted between males, for reason that these
> relations are culturally taboo, are rerouted through the figure of
> the woman and, through representation, at the expense of women.
> This is one of those ways that the visual field operates, and some
> of these aspects of pornography—certainly the depictions you're
> responding to—may decidedly not be about female satisfaction,
> but rather satisfaction between men over women. And women
> may play into these positions.

> There's a framing and framing-out of self/other, rational/irrational,
> masculine/feminine, in order to constitute a chain of hierarchies.
> There are also parallel logics of inclusion/exclusion that may
> underwrite desires for consensus, and which might penalize

difference, despite how progressive we might claim to be. If we as subjects want to be porous, rather than shielded and shut down to each other, I think we have to be very careful to not deny the contingency that this interrelationality manifests.

It might be misleading to stake intimacy entirely on any one assessment. Even from inside a situation, we have to remember that understanding doesn't rule out misunderstanding. There might be blind spots.

Are you speaking about the symbolizations of opportunities for penetration as being impossible invitations, false binaries?

In the worst case, rather than allowing for an encounter with difference, there's an attempt to overcome it. There's no interpenetration. Paradoxically, it's all intercourse without intercourse!

I also believe something different is happening in the private images, but again these competing readings, distinct as they are, are left open to bleeding into each other . . .

I think we need to speak directly about the repeated and significant presence of pornographic imagery in *Double Bind*—spreads, scenarios as well as single images, from porn magazines, straight and gay, of various genres and sources.

Many of these are also not hardcore, however—at least not nearly as brutal, for instance, as the pairings of pornography and countercultural or theoretical sources that appear violently against each other in my collaboration with Nicolás Guagnini.[3]

Even so, they're intense. Is this to show the extremes of where the ideology of patriarchy can go? Is it to make the exceptional-woman image, the image of the available feminine ideal that we associate with Meghan, is it to enframe that imagery in a nonpalliative way . . . ? If I walked around the installation, I could collect quite a few of these extreme moments from the public print-media collection, where the

female body and its orifices are photographed and presented as an
isolated and dehumanized penetration palace.

> It does function as a negation in that sense. Maintaining this
> inconclusiveness, I want to propose that this mass-media
> pornography in *Double Bind* may also speak to an additional set
> of cultural conflicts or oppositions. First, I see it associated with
> so-called low-culture's desire for kitsch, and its pitting of the sexual
> or the kitsch against authoritarian high-cultural controls and
> exclusions. I'm thinking about how countercultural movements
> have attempted to harness negative affects to redraw the symbolic,
> values established by older generations, for instance; but also,
> and perhaps more problematically, of the popular mass media's
> punitive use of exposure—the use of Murdoch-style tabloid fodder
> to pollute high values. In some cases, this stripping of clothes may
> have as much to do with the stripping of decorum, or even the
> stripping of position. Internal to the erotic-fantasy constructions,
> there might be more than just erotics at play. These aspects might
> be heavily entwined with class fantasies or aversions that the
> pornographic is intended to level. I also sense that advertising
> exploits this assumed Freudian binary—Freud's theory of drives
> and desire set against cultural controls. This repression model
> functions as the prerequisite for transgression, liberation sold to us
> in terms of instant gratification.

I view the inclusion of pornographic imagery in *Double Bind* as
a move against the contradictions of Freudian binaries that hold
the sexual drive as either liberated or repressed, with repression
largely defining desire. Not to mention that since the 2000s and
the Internet, it's hard to position the pornographic gaze and
pornography as a way of viewing and an industry that is repressed
in our society. On the contrary, it sticks to everything, every image
seems to have a pornographic source behind it, there are direct
references and borrowings, these are ubiquitous . . .

> But this is also one reason why staging this conversation about
> how the private interpenetrates the public is so important. There's
> the claim that the virtual is the site of pathology. Here we touch on

the regulation of appearances, and the subsequent excess left over from that process of regulating. What starts to publicly appear, to be destigmatized or even naturalized, due to the preponderance of its collective practice online, for instance? It seems much of this is buffered through the visual.

There are also specific temporal and cultural references within the media materials, where within certain eras distinct attitudes or tastes are shared more or less openly, or aggressively and so forth, and these shift. So a person's actions might come to be understood or else misunderstood later.

There might be another way into this: fantasy construction. Couldn't the pornographic be present so emphatically here in order to fill out the psychic, fantasy-based, wishful layers?

Maybe there is something about this promise of a promiscuity of positions. It makes me want to emphasize, however, an ethics that's necessary if one is to dabble there. This question of individuating oneself, while necessary, is actually a risky proposition—it's highly open to failure. And because it involves a destabilization of one's subjectivity, which means that it also has the potential to be contagious to others, this might be met with control.

I think *Double Bind* may be searching after another theory of external life and the internal, interiority, one that sees the necessary rejection of the way feminist tools blocked the psychic workings of sexism and its self-internalization, and which reproduces the Freudian repression/liberation logic. I am thinking of the work of figures who have been controversial and not well understood in this regard, such as the Sylvia Plath that Jacqueline Rose's reading brought out so vividly: the position that's creative, treats the contradictions as lived, accepts complicities as the everyday thinking-through of social and cultural life, and understands writing as a place to stage these implications, of which exaggeration is a part.

I agree. We can't pretend that one person's performance of self-objectification might mean exactly the same thing as someone else's. Because that use of the self is tactical, it's also contingent, and it strikes me that these dynamics can only ever be observed indirectly, speculatively, but also that they must be read very closely. We can't simply overlay meanings from outside. At least subjectively, meaning is localized: the product of the possible decisions from any given position, plus the horizon of possibilities that any decision opens onto.

Maybe from that speculative point, I can turn to Meghan's images and think, for her part, that she may be very knowing about role-play and exaggeration.

One observation that stays with me is that the way the panels approach collage or other art forms may lead us on a pathway that is not very relevant. Essentially, it's not about a figure/ground, or a beneath, or even about what's inside the frame or pairs of frames. It's more of a theatrical model that is being proposed. It is risky to position a work this way, to allow for the contradictions, to give them their locality of context, as you say, action and reaction, to make a theater of that reveal—risky because it rubs against expectations for so-called critical art.

3. *Anna and Carl and Some Other Couples*, a collaboration between Ledare and Nicolás Guagnini that was first exhibited at Andrew Roth, New York, February 13–March 14, 2014. The project combines a printout of a *New York Times* article of February 12, 1988 (one of the well-known items of press coverage of the legal case in which artist Carl Andre was accused and acquitted of pushing his wife, artist Ana Mendieta, to her death from a window of their Greenwich Village apartment) with 126 books (various titles from the humanities and social sciences). The books have been cut with circular holes. Inset into the books' holes are images from a pornography archive that dates from the 1960s–1970s. A publication was created that contains the project's elements in the form of an artists' book and a new element: a design with a black circle which grows larger in diameter as the book's pages progress until the pages are solid black. This black aperture suggests a camera, and manifests the book's hybrid book-object status, since the book can be unbound and arranged on the wall following the measurements of the aperture.

III.

RHEA ANASTAS: Meghan is framing herself and being framed in multiple ways, ways that aren't always comfortable to see or to think about. The viewer is in this way implicated. One assumption may be that each role played out in the project is staging a position on culture as it comes across in imagery of this kind. Can we also assume that these positions are critical?

The narrative description for the work given in the handwritten script that introduces the installation situates your and Adam's roles as photographers of an intimate relation—as husbands. So the viewer takes in the roles in the imagery as actual, as lived.

I am thinking about the ways critique is employed in relation to contemporary art, and I come up against an interesting problem: What if the art that is routinely taken as exposing, or involved in deconstructing in order to read politics, etc., what if its function is not actually the activity that *Double Bind* performs? What if the model isn't about art that reads the culture, but how certain values and frameworks, even expectations, are carried by the work, reproducing and communicating cultural codes as such, carrying them over into and as the work? Would we then have to position *Double Bind*'s photographic imagery, and the collage panels as media imagery, differently? This brings me to the question of how to conceptualize the social address being activated.

LEIGH LEDARE: Well, on one hand, culture moves through individual subjects. It's reproduced through us, and through our communications, and we might ask ourselves whether our relationship to this is active or passive, or try to approach this nondualistically. Not dismissing those critical ambitions, it's a question of how the work performs, right? Does the work live as a report of a process—or does it constitute an active process, and how might that activate a viewer? How as receivers might we be made to attune ourselves to the work, and how are questions of consent or refusal wrapped into this?

I wonder what you mean by *attunement*?

By placing the viewer into a space of lived relations, affects, and responses, and by not didactically predigesting this experience, not telling the viewer what to think, *Double Bind* puts forward a set of stakes. The viewer is subjected to a parallel set of problems as enacted inside the work, making them responsible to sort out a position for themselves. Distinct from the certainty of cerebral, analytic overlays, it casts criticality as unfolding, as inconclusive and subjective, and also as limited, as something which in order to be authentic has to be continuously activated and reengaged.

I think we have to question the claims of so-called critical art and look at what kinds of movements are possible within subjectification and subjectivity, to ask how agency is located in the management of means-and-ends systems, ever so subtly changing this subject/control/apparatus structuralism into a context where feedback and stylization and self-fashioning may matter, where they can shape and recreate.

I would not want to define the art of this in terms of a corrective, morally or politically better imagery, not at all. We can agree on that.

I see these conditions you speak about as critical considerations within specific situations and contexts. They are unfolding and in need of being activated.

You've already spoken about how as a viewer you experience ambivalence encountering the performances, photographs, and other materials of *Double Bind*. I want to bring up another aspect of these images: the possibility that one might enjoy them, but also not enjoy the fact of enjoying them, or be caught off guard by her own response. My ambivalence mirrors yours, but I also can't deny that the seduction of these image types functions on me. I'm also split. And perhaps I even like being split. At the same time that I locate a feminist approach as a primary origin and source for me in making this piece—positioning stereotypes front and center—the specific relationship that I'm taking up in *Double Bind* is purposefully complicated. Why choose not to withdraw from

participating in something that's so obviously problematic? It's also
a fallacy to believe we aren't complicit.

There may be a pleasure, that's one contradiction. But before going
headlong into feminist tools and problematics, I want to know to
what degree the viewer can assume that each of the participants'
positions are critical—is this something the viewer has reference
points for within the work, within viewing?

> As much as the theoretical, I'm interested in an empirical
> experience of the work—in fact, I don't see these as necessarily
> separate. The viewer can't come to the project without some
> preformed feelings about romantic love or marriage or intimacy
> (with all their dependencies and conflicts), and the issues
> around their representation, let alone the lived experience
> of subjectification, self-objectification, and the psychological
> dynamics that the photographic performances generate.

> My work is not about overlaying a morally authoritative message,
> but describing a set of contradictions, respecting that each viewer
> will uniquely experience those conflicts which *Double Bind* raises.
> The function of this is to force a questioning of how the visual
> field operates, even considering our willful nonrecognition of how
> through the visual field we're made complicit and submitted to
> these contradictions.

I want to pause just to ask you what you mean by the visual field.
Is this what we see of the performances and in the framed panels?
I just want to be clear, since to me the photographs that came out
of the two encounters in the cabin can't really be comprehended in
positivistic terms.

> I am referring to the primacy of sight, and how it's predominantly
> through sight, through the framing and functionalizing of
> perspective, that we define power relationships and limits. This
> often happens through a kind of sleight of hand, something akin
> to a shell game. We fall back on visual and bodily language to
> express much of what can't be said verbally: to articulate desires,

fears, shame, and emotion sideways because of the risks we encounter in addressing these directly. The point is to amplify existing antagonisms that we might not want to recognize—not in order to alienate, but to see them as complements rather than opposites, as related.

You also seem to be very interested in how all sorts of information that may not be directly communicated or made reference to—how details, detailing—is handled and played out through social behavior. Take a specific context—your trip with Meghan, let's say. What's possible to be communicated within the parameters of that time spent together? What can boundaries contain or restrain, what can they allow to be put out corporeally?

I wonder, what are the cues for the viewer? And what was your actual process of structuring this within the performances? Did you have a way of trying to get this detailing out of the interactions and the photography that accompanied them?

> *Double Bind*'s script orders the performances, but it also opens the installation, introducing a set of parameters for viewing and focusing the viewer on what to pay attention to. The question of difference raised by the comparative structure is key. First, as a response to an observed dynamic, I created the script. This was an abstract model—a system that the subjective parts, the participants in the project, were then submitted to. The actions of the specific participants, including mine, fleshed out the script. So, at the initial level, this was about an ordering of the complexity of the environment. This structuring created the conditions for the internal complexity that plays out interrelationally—at the level of the individual participants' agency, at the psychosocial level. The script functions as a kind of container. It's a framing—not unlike that of the camera, but on an interrelational scale that allows for a recording and mapping of these cross-reflective dynamics.

In viewing I hold an open place for all this detailing of what can't be stated, of the performances and the internal complications within each scenario, and how some of this crosses from one situation into the other. The photographs suggest that a cataloguing of these worlds of privacy could be taking place. But the indexical can't actually do this, nor can the relationships between each couple. I am left with the sense, as you just put it, of what to pay attention to, what kinds of experience, but my attention is in a strange way overloaded on a sensory level, and at the same time disappointed, because I can't get to this experience, I can't see it—and the participants' experience is parallel, they can and can't get to it, too. In *Double Bind* something extremely subjective turns around and looks at times to be highly objective. It conjures the discourse of the archive, the objectification of daily life, but here, in *Double Bind*'s so-called archive, the capturing of affect and encounters would always be that which fills in this objectification, and that which is missing from it.

> That's partly what I mean by emphasizing that *Double Bind*'s meaning hinges on this projective space.

Will you read the project description?

> It reads: "*Double Bind*. Convince my ex-wife to go alone with me for three nights to a remote cabin, upstate NY. Married for five years, but now divorced for five years. She agrees, but gets remarried before we leave. I stay with her and photograph her over the course of the four days. This results in roughly 500 images. We sleep in different beds. Most time we've spent together in five years. Two months later, pay for Meghan to return with current husband to the same cabin. Three nights again. He also happens to be a photographer. Photographs her for four days, brings me fourteen rolls of unprocessed film. I process and print all 1,000 photographs over the course of the next ten days. This results in two sets of images. My images of my ex-wife appear on black; his images of his new wife appear on white. This makes up the first comparative structure. The two sets of photographs are then positioned against a collection of media images and other ephemera. This makes up the second comparative structure."

So the main contours of the comparative structures, the two

overlapping ones, are introduced: the first, the triangle created
through the recording of the two relationships; and the second
having to do with the cross-reading of these private images of
Meghan with the juxtaposed public images from the
media collection.

> These problematics don't simply originate with my constructing
> the script though—it's a rematerialization and description of
> dynamics that preexist it, and which are contemporaneous and
> intertwined with culture, right? Such dynamics are already
> overwhelmingly present in the collection of media materials.

But the text—it's not entirely straightforward, is it? You're using a
voice, and one of the things that you do in the course of the script
is to share a certain amount of information that's autobiographical—
it is offered as such, within the narrative voice anyway. Even so,
I don't know where exactly to place that voice, how to read the
telling: autobiographical and distilled down, conceptualist in
some sense.

There are a few areas of heavily-marked redactions in the writing
in the project description. The reader is reminded of how much she
doesn't know, and of what is visible and invisible.

Another thing that you do is gesture in a really condensed way
toward fantasy construction. Since only a few details appear, they
command a certain attention, such as "convince my ex-wife," and
"she agrees, but gets remarried before we leave," and "we sleep in
different beds."

> Well, something might first be said about the notion of a self—a
> constructed object related to ego which can be held onto—and
> how this differs from the notion of a subject, which is rooted in
> phenomenological experience.

> As soon as one reads the script, one has to ask oneself: Where does
> the voice stand? How is this something that remains slippery?
> How is the viewer unable to situate herself clearly in relationship

to surface-level readings of the script? Even if *Double Bind* centers the viewer on certain types of relations, there's still a difference between the ideological frame and how we attune ourselves to its delivery. Performance may also have this necessarily aberrant relationship to its own referent, each of which act to mutually pervert the other, one thing disordering the other.

You mean that this relationship to the referent and the meaning of the performance is dissonant and shifting? Actually, I wanted to stay on the writing for a moment . . .

Okay, well you're also pointing to something more that's at play here—what could maybe be described as a tactical self-objectification, the positioning of this self as an object posed site-specifically or contextually. This uses autobiography to frame identification at the same time as it confounds autobiography, and plays with it, not unlike what in literary criticism might be described as unreliable narration. It's a problem of how one must bring oneself into alignment with the very thing one is confronted by. And here we're talking about language, systems of signifiers, cultural facts, and affects.

So the exposure of the mechanisms of your own acts of concealment are nested inside your performance of self-implication, and it's partially how this is delivered that's so surprising. It's highly destabilizing, and as a viewer the intersubjectivity of the piece is also unreliable, made unsafe—I can't know exactly where I stand because I don't know exactly where you stand, and there's something extremely anxiety producing (and productive) about how this positions me. It strikes me that this is a kind of trigger, one that mirrors the movements of what I myself as a viewer might also prefer to reason myself out of or to keep concealed.

I'm also trying to get at the technique of opening with this project description as a framing device. Did you have a version of the project description that was just the facts?

As far as I'm concerned, the voice is factual, but it's factual like a photograph, and that in and of itself isn't so cut and dry. It can't escape having elements of artifice.

The viewer realizes quickly that the script's stereotypes can't be read straight—they're literally queered. At the same time, this position—what Judith Butler might call the performative—really collapses with the experienced facts of our lives, even though we are performing as/in these real roles. It's because these are literal relations we're enacting, and it's that explicit performative utterance that is being staged, that makes us complicit. Despite the vulnerability and discomfort of returning to this relationship, it is in fact what I am doing, it is what each participant is doing. We're each subjecting ourselves to the script in order to speak back to the structural relations that underwrite the stereotypes we're occupying. And we're addressing the viewer with all the consequences that come with that, as subjects, as objects, and as witnesses.

This subjective address, this declarative "I," announces a specific dynamic. It's intersubjective and initiates an intimacy that would be neutralized if addressed through the third person. It grates, and as a viewer I may want to not want it. *Double Bind*'s narrative asks the participants to perform attachments and relational investments that fall clearly within these heteronormative cultural models, that are disagreeable to the social milieu to which they're addressed. Because it's attached to somebody—specifically to you—and because of the conventions of responsibility around authorship, this you as a subject is provided for me as a site to attribute the symptomatic. There's something very important in this: you providing yourself as a target, as something I can capture and frame, also allows me to attribute to you an intensity of feelings and hurts and so forth, one that exceeds your own complicity in the piece, that is accentuated through the confrontation with all this media material, and which for me I internalize in a way that becomes quite personal, as though you are actually enacting something on me. I have to stop then and remind myself also that everyone who's taken part in the project has openly agreed to do so.

Are you suggesting that intimacy might be something that exceeds
this rational or conceptual identification with the types of images
Double Bind is appropriating and producing?

The idea of the event or encounter may be important. The lived
part, too. There is the sense that interrelations, actions, and reactions
between the three of you are set up as soon as you approach
Meghan with your idea for the two trips. On the articulated level,
Meghan and Adam agree. But things also happen on the level
of action, behaviors . . . like, they get married two weeks before
Meghan's date to travel to the cabin with you comes around. This
doesn't seem like a coincidence.

I wasn't aware of their plans, when they would marry, but I knew
they were engaged. But it also put our relations in a certain light. I
was also in another long-term relationship.

The work is acting on all of you already, before the photographing
even begins . . . This carries over to the viewer.

As for me, I know there's something more, and I have to resist my
own desires that well up, particularly the response of wanting to
isolate causes that may categorize what the piece does, and what you
do, as though it was doing it to me directly as I was standing there
viewing, not necessarily wanting to view that—Meghan's beauty and
presence performed as such with the two husbands, or projected
as such, or the media images and their recurring subordinations.
This puts me in the position of placing Meghan or that imagery as
a target or thing I have to disobey. Or as an idea that I have to be
skeptical about, the project description. How do I manage what I
may see as an element of cruelty, one which you both enact with the
camera, another that's enacted on Meghan and Adam through the
interpersonal, injecting something from your past into their
new relationship?

All this manifests these feelings in a way that is unpleasant but
which I realize also, importantly, opens up a space for thought. But
to do that is extremely destabilizing and challenging. Especially

because the conceptual space I end up modeling diverges from the typical one constructed by feminist tools: expose sexual difference, uncover male domination as such. This equation between sexuality and the patriarchy is rather rigid. What about pleasure? Feminist analyses can be problematic for what they reify and fix, unable to register possible investments, acts of complicity . . .

> Well, yeah, that's one aspect of an approach such as this. It's like someone's car alarm going off repeatedly in the middle of the night! Even once it ends you're still haunted by it, knowing it can reerupt any time.

Another characteristic of the work is that it asks us to not simply decode it from the safe vantage of our own interiority. Instead, it pushes us around, pushes us to respond. While the performances are initially staged for the camera, as objects and as an installation *Double Bind* also stages and generates contingencies, engaging the viewer in a theater of identifications and disobediences and asking for something more.

That speaks to another question: *Pretend You're Actually Alive*, which looked closely at your mother's self-presentation, likewise employed photographs, narrative elements, documents or pseudodocuments, and ephemera from your family history. Did you have to work with a family member in *Double Bind*? It seems important that you realized this project with Meghan; who, I should mention, also appears in a few photographs in *Pretend You're Actually Alive*.

> There's this recursive aspect, where each subsequent work functions to redefine or complicate former projects, so there's this chain of significations that extend through bodies of work. Each also comments back on the legacies I've inherited, and on the modes or mediums used.

> In the case of *Double Bind*, the performances accumulate force in dialogue with my other work, but also based on the stakes of those existing intimacies and established patterns of trust between

the parties. Here, there's also a writing-back into the discursive history of photographic documentary practice, and especially the practice of artists who work with their partners, families, or subcultures—how the notion of self-portraiture applied to one's own social milieu has been used to gloss over asymmetries in agency, or conditions of voyeurism inherent in representation. In vernacular photography and art both, sexual imagery dovetails with this in complex ways, often acting in line with more positivistic, self-expressive claims. These claims function as a blind for the potentially coercive roles that intimacy might play, but also cast these acts of stylization in terms of subject/culture rather than modes of intersubjective signification between subjects.

What does that mean for you within photography? Can you break that down for me? Can you lay out how you're using photography differently in *Double Bind*?

What's at stake in *Double Bind* isn't photography as much as it's performativity, but also the phenomenological understanding of the visual. For instance, how we might display intimacy to underwrite a proof of intimacy, or how we might record, construct, and circulate ourselves socially as objects through images. Most vernacular photography constructs appearances within this means-ends logic.

But the nature of the singular still photograph is that there's this inherent limitation: it presents a façade, it's one fragment bracketed off from a longer expanse of time. And severed from context, it can't speak directly to the conversations that may have taken place around the image, nor can it make apparent the histories or inevitable ambitions that the subjects are invested in. Nor can it attest to how the viewer's projection floods in, or how discourse directs those responses.

But photography is still the primary material vehicle through which *Double Bind* occurs.

I see *Double Bind*'s medium per se as social, interrelational, and intersubjective. I am approaching photography through this lens, employing it as a feedback mechanism in order to look at how image relations imbricate human relations. The visual field comprises a medium through which all these psychosocial dynamics play out. What I'm trying to do in using this networked model of authorship, and by showing images in this quantity, through these two cuts of time, is to anchor how their meaning is contingent on, and emerges through, this constellation of relations.

There's always this excess that lies beyond appearances, and that allows for a representation to occur. This is what *Double Bind*'s comparative structure and the diptychs that diagram its relations try to encircle and rematerialize.

I can see where *Double Bind* borrows from conceptualist traditions of deskilling, of privileging the capacity of the camera to record, but that also points to the issues of control that emerge alongside the negation of the singular photographic perspective, and through the management structures that this distribution of authorship puts into play. Can that still be seen as counter to how photography is typically used?

I think Vilém Flusser summed this up really well in his description of the photographer as a functionary of the camera or apparatus. So, it's the subject who is being used by technology, rather than the other way around. Flusser argued that the active role of the photographer is to rupture the existing possibilities of the program by creating new information—the paradox being that whatever new information is created is inevitably recouped by the apparatus, expanding and bolstering its program, and in the process hollowing out the finite combinations open to the photographer. Flusser recognized that this horizon of logic is tied to the information/control society brought about by our dependencies on technology and various apparati, and he links this to the camera's function in the production of what he coins "technical images." The implication is that the radical emancipatory potential that modernization's emphasis on technological evolution claimed for itself is anything but emancipatory. He paints this as a dystopia—our condition as subjects increasingly limited and totalized through our interpolation, absorption, and production of technological and informational control.

So the framing of consciousness is what is at stake here, and Flusser's really claiming that the program manages, recoups, and monopolizes individual consciousness and those excesses or even affects that might trouble the apparatus.

My question about such totalizing critiques that are pitched to the systemic scale—a scale counter to *Double Bind*, from the point of view of the subject and subjectivity—is that there can be expressions of agency, and there can be what Sedgwick calls the "middle ranges" of agency, and it is here where she locates doing, as in creative acts and potential change.

In a way, you're right: Flusser is so caught up in the system-centric, as opposed to subject-centric, problems of these communications models and apparatus theory. And in de-emphasizing the subjective, he also takes a distinctly anticontent stance, arguing that under the autopoiesis of the apparatus human intention and agency fall out.

Well, that could scarcely suffice for your work. Not to turn to a traditional term, but it's loaded with subject matter, with bodies!

Okay, partly. At the same time, Flusser's thought holds this contradiction: he places emphasis on a phenomenological viewpoint, one that takes into account the experience (and functioning) of the subject relative to her contingency within an apparatus or social system.

The self-reflexive turn of contemporary practices, Flusser really doesn't account for this. In addition, and this is undoubtedly a minor point, I also think the functionalism or interpellation that *Double Bind* puts forward may be a different one than Flusser's, one that might actually be framing Flusser's model, but also creating an opening for something we can think of as agency. But I already described why totalizing views are less crucial to what we're conceptualizing here: the affective and relational realm of subjects understood in more material conditions, specificities, layered details, and psychological terms.

> Where Flusser is extremely clear is that he refuses to pretend that we actually have more agency than we do, and that disempowerment he describes is purposeful—I have to take it as a provocation. I also think the severity of his reaction has to be understood against Habermas's social-justice model, which overemphasizes the opposite: a liberal-humanist, human-centric agency. But despite these ways in which Flusser frames his argument, for me it all revolves around this gap—a question about the subject and of what might exceed the scripting of the subject, and a question about the lacunae where agency might be found.
>
> Within an interrelational model there are multiple valences that have to be accounted for, and this also functions to destabilize the fixity of intentions, but in a way that likewise challenges Flusser's assumptions. This is accentuated by the contingency, a double contingency, of the participants—who are doubly blind, in the sense that not only is it impossible for them to know what each other are truly thinking or experiencing, but, similarly, it's impossible for any subject to comprehend the full spectrum of her own intentions, desires, and responses in any single moment. Intentionality resides in a different place here, within a space of projection and transference—it's speculative. It's as if to say: "maybe we meant this, but from another angle, maybe we meant something completely different . . ." How might we simultaneously be both inside and outside our intentions or motivations and the apparatus? From there, the question is: We know there are ways in which the limits and capacities of what is given can be tested as the subject manages these contradictions, we can attest to contradiction, but can this lead us to a capacity to act?

In *Double Bind*, one participant's motivations and potentials to act within its situation are always kind of tethered to and modified by others. It's so detailed, the interior of this part of the piece. I return again and again to ask, where is the viewer in this? She is a kind of control for the outside, for the objective function. That said, the detailed arena of identifications that *Double Bind* builds up—it resubjectifies, cloaking the viewer in the same haze of contingencies.

> This movement of subjectivity within existent conditions is a better vocabulary than resistance: it's the material and psychological milieu you're talking about.

I'm not sure. It could be psychological, and could be showing an ontological quality at the same time, don't you think?

> This management of being subjectified, an emergent response that comes through the situation and its feedback, offers a possible shift of our investments and positionalities within the symbolic: agency could be activated here. While Flusser emphasized the role of innovation, he failed to anticipate how repetition might be taken up as the artistic move par excellence, not toward innovation but as a tactic of reframing and recontextualizing, a process of resignification whose meaning is wholly dependent on the multiple contexts through which it's coded and understood.

There's a way it seems to me that feminist critiques in the context of experimental or avant-garde art wanted both to turn the apparatus back on itself—wanted that high-degree of reflexivity as a politics and an ethos—but also had to speak about positionality itself as caught up in the patriarchy and its modes of authorization or self-authorization. Repetition, I guess as an attention to positionality, leads to seeing or reading institutional and discursive conditions— overdeterminations of sexual difference for artists and viewers, through gender, let's say, and in diverse other ways.

> De Certeau said something about the tactical, suggesting that any victory is a victory that has to be given back. The implication is that communication is premised on difference—a certain thing has to be distinct from another thing, and those distinctions might rest as much on who's using that thing and for what, as on how that difference is being used as a means of ordering our relationality.

How Meghan is understood in *Double Bind* from the space of two distinct vantages exemplifies this, but it's also through her that my and Adam's relative positions are ordered, our relations to inclusion and exclusion, and so on. Communication might also be about noncommunication or opacity: difference in that case being used toward a kind of coding, inevitably a controlling of who has access or not. And, as I've said, it's important to recognize that understanding doesn't rule out misunderstanding. Here we come up against a situation in which, while we may attribute a certain degree of intentionality to a subject, there's always a counter condition in which individual intentionality hits a limit and is acted upon by another. It's not monodirectional, but is transformed by system.

What we've been discussing up until now could fall under the framework and strategies of *enactment*. So maybe now is a good moment to discuss enactment as a method, and its relationship to photography. I want to emphasize that enactment may relate to the resignification that you were just considering, but that it does this without language per se or exclusively, even if we use language to talk about it. It's staged and posed, though where the part taken from life ends and the designing, narrativizing, and acting begin, these can't easily be separated. As a technique and idea, enactment comes up a lot in body-based performance, dance, improvisation in music, but also in video and film work. In its simplest form, enactment repeats a story or encounter or trauma or a pattern within a history, relationship, or family dynamic, and the term is also used in psychology and psychoanalytic contexts to examine such dynamics and treat them through actually acting the relationship out in therapy, so the therapy has this empirical, reflexive aspect. Enactment doesn't really have a place within photographic discourse—it's a relatively recent concept for us to think about inside of photography, or within art that uses photography.

Because most photography is approached in terms of images rather than systems.

Undoubtedly.

> Enactment allows a subject to inhabit a position, and through
> doing so it traces out the patterns that operate within the
> interpersonal relational context, and these of course relate more
> broadly to culture. The idea is to apply pressure to these patterns
> in order to sound them out. It functions as a kind of diagnostic
> exercise for making these patterns visible. Enactment creates a
> situation that doubles, and therefore maps, an existing situation
> or structure, even a pattern of seeing things. In small, subtle ways,
> it reveals itself to be parodying its object, calling it into question
> at a fundamental level. In this way a gap is created between the
> acceptance of those structures as naturalized, and an understanding
> of them as constructions whose meaning is contingent.

> Enactment hinges on this use of the self and its attachments. It
> uses that contingency, the subjective, to get under and inside
> the logic of structures, to question the orthodoxies of certain
> positions. Enactment is about the particular. It has to do with the
> functionality of the object or subject within specific conditions,
> and this collapsing of the representational and the literal. In *Double
> Bind*, enactment situates its subjects, including myself and the
> viewer, amidst and between these competing cultural sentiments.
> There's a mapping of incompatible contexts, competing
> understandings of a singular event that can't be reconciled, which
> creates a kind of vertigo.

Let's break it down in terms of how the shooting events actually
worked. You and Meghan traveled in July 2009, and produced your
photographs together first?

Two months after that first trip, in September, Meghan and Adam
made their weekend trip and photographs. Adam hadn't seen your
images. Meghan had made these with you, but hadn't seen the
actual negatives or contact sheets, right? When you photograph
with Meghan before they do, you are located in your present
relationship, and might be looking back at a past version of
your relationship. Then, with Meghan taking something of that

experience with her, let's speculate, this becomes a reference point of some kind within the shooting that they do; the relationships can be seen in this way in parallel. The structure makes it so.

> As the newlywed, Adam is cast in a position that I occupied ten years prior. Fictionally speaking, the repetition of enactment shifts from my figure to his, from the dyad of one couple to another. It's amplified, because the straight therapy idea of enactment considers the subject with her tendency to recreate the qualities of prior relationships or roles in present relationships. Or the inverse, my position as Meghan's husband anticipates his position ten years on.

It's a mirroring in this case. Its also interrelational as opposed to singular, since the dyads cross, and may speak to larger social structures, in this sense beyond the boundedness of the participants' psychology.

> Exactly . . . there's this overlapping of the psychic space of fantasy, which, like memory, exists in a kind of omnipresent way. Or, if nothing else, it erupts on its own schedule, involuntarily, and this is triggered through the encounters that *Double Bind* stages. I'd qualify, however, what you said a few minutes ago: we need to recognize that Meghan emphatically *does* bring something along with her, but also that we can't know exactly what that is. It's a gap.

> This is where the primary distinction between enactment and performance lies. Enactment isn't simply a performance or reperformance of something, but a submitting of oneself to a structure through which the subject undergoes something that actually might modify them. This stake is crucial—that collapsing of (or slipping between) performance and reality. It's both a lack of distancing, an implication, and at the same time it takes a peculiar distance, in that it refuses to mediate the viewer's moral and ethical responses.

This is the space you were referring to, where projection and speculation flood in . . .

People have expressed surprise that my interaction with Meghan actually comes across as far more intimate than what is pictured in the images of her made by Adam. Perhaps this has to do with perceptions the viewer has about the intensity of my emotional and conceptual investments in the project and this repetition— there's that quote, but I've forgotten now who said it: "Consistency in contradiction measures the force of a desire."

It's important to watch what we attribute to this arena, how we describe and limit the openness of that gap, which exceeds what the image can present. It's also the space of transference, and our interpretations might actually say a lot about how we attempt to smooth over contradictions and difference, how we make assumptions to serve our own ends, overlaying our own singular and fixed perspectives across conditions that are actually multiple and temporal and more complex than we account for.

What made you decide to script it so that you went first, and what's the importance of your going first?

The vestiges of my former relationship with Meghan are staged as a potential interruption coming forward into their current relationship. Next, Meghan and Adam's images perform a transformation, or variation, or even a writing-back into that first trip that Meghan had taken with me—and maybe from Adam's perspective, an overwriting. The entire project contains all these multiple framings at the level of time and scale, even extending backward or projecting forward in time. These actions are problematizations and power plays made by the participants, problematizations of problematizations.

That was just stated narrowly, from your point of view, the potential interruption. Just like I can't know Meghan's motivations, that gap, or the narrowing or partiality that seems to emerge from speaking into the complexity, that is interesting. It's so unstable.

What were you going for when you were shooting? Were there deliberate ways that you approached this?

In terms of my photographing Meghan, I tried to allow this extended space and duration, and the repetition and redundancy of the image-making, to take over. This unfolded slowly through a conversation that we both shaped. A lot of this is about hanging out in what psychoanalysis might call "primary position," with the conditions and camera creating this hyperreflexive awareness that each of us is performing, enacting, and, in turn, signifying.

Meghan had some partial sense of what her images with Adam were going to be from having produced them with you.

Well, Meghan also has agency within the production of the second set, which she produced with Adam, but also, at least somewhat, produced for me, alongside everything that's being signified to me through these images, and with how she's using herself to frame me. She's the only internal witness to (and actor in) both events, and she's problematizing the problematization that I set up for her, just as Adam's doing the same with me, and I with Adam. Our positions are intertwined, transitioning from the subjective to the social and structural, back to the subjective.

As I've said, there's a way that the camera is presented as a feedback mechanism, with its function to record and transmit information—and through this, its making present of the absent third party as the necessary witness to each trip. This sets up the conditions for Meghan to tactically assert herself. Each trip (and each relationship) is distinct, but is also a counterpoint for the other. Meghan positions herself relative to each of us, and through each of us to the other.

On the level of communication, in order for feedback to function, there needs to be this witness. It can't fulfill its role, in other words it can't actually *feed back*, unless there's this form of regarding and assessment that comes alongside the facts of the event. It's the witness (both as participant and as viewer) who activates this interrelationality.

And that's the difference between an open system and a closed one. Adam and I serve as witnesses for each other, but Meghan also employs each of us as witness, and then there's this augmented awareness of the viewer. In each instance, it's through the function of that outside observer that inside these situations we're allowed to fully understand the scope of our actions and positions, and to actively construct agency through our negotiation of these structures. Similarly, without being able to experience this through an outside observer, we can't attune ourselves to the sets of meanings put in play.

I would emphasize that the witnessing position for each of you whose lives the work is about, and which you're self-exposing and performing, and that for the viewer, who is positioned at a remove, have differences.

Well, sure, meaning stems from these direct encounters, too, from being inside that situation cognitively. It absolutely does, but the meaning of this reality is contingent, it continues to unfold and increase in complexity and relationally. Also, in order for me to reexperience it, it's necessary to do this vicariously through the viewer's eyes, and in relation to their contingency—there's that division of selfhood that allows us to see ourselves from outside ourselves. It's almost like a joke, in that once you know the punch line in order to appreciate the surprise you need that outside party who isn't yet filled in.

Okay, but did you know what to expect from the shooting scenario?

Honestly, no. And I didn't know what feelings I would experience. The structure produced what it produced—it visually mapped each relationship. The only parameters I gave Adam were to minimize technical and formal differences: to photograph with a 50 mm or 35 mm lens, on black-and-white film. Minimizing that noise made it possible to focus the comparison on what was being performed differently in each of the two trips. It was also a way of draining or bringing things down to a documentary model, on one hand, while on the other saving this other formal device, black and white versus color, to maintain the distinction between private images and public media.

What is complicated to sort through, to read, but also to experience, is that aspect that has Meghan look as if she is making herself conform to imagery that may not be in her self-interest. Using her possession of beauty and a sexual image, what to women can look like a form of power within their reach, also rests completely along the lines of a male fantasy, of containment within this.

> But also, to make Meghan alone bear responsibility for her role, to frame her involvement to that totalizing extent, is a severe and perhaps less-compassionate form of constraint. We can't only assume she's being used, as opposed to using the situation or getting something out of it herself.

Getting one thing out of this, despite another dynamic that is not of her choosing. That's what the mass-media images are doing, to show what roles are scripted for us, for women, by patriarchy.

> Possibly, yes. However, that overlay of an analysis that prohibits self-objectification, which reduces it to a symptom, also ignores the weight of these social contracts and her negotiation of them.

> There's this insistent question of utility: How is each of us using the structure? This is the political within enactment. Paradoxically, her agreeing to participate in *Double Bind* may have as much to do with asserting her autonomy within her new marriage with Adam, for instance, as it does with her desires to be an object of admiration, or to seek validation from me before moving forward; even to regulate our roles relative to her own, to create this dynamic of rivalry as proof of affection. It may also be about her making amends for something. At least psychologically speaking, it may be as much for her as for Adam or myself.

> I also can't discount my own personal, psychological motivations, some of which, being unconscious, I'm necessarily unaware. Enactment carries this messiness. Then, and still now, it's impossible to fully know the exact intentions and unconscious dilemmas that we were acting out. Psychoanalysis teaches us that, that there's always a speculative and projective aspect of experience.

It's also linked to poiesis, this kind of shifting and redefining of visual language, or the redefinition of the present through a reemergence of prior experience, the transmutation of all these unconscious affects and forms.

What further structuring of the project did you consider once you saw what Adam's photographs looked like? Did you use the fact that Adam is a fashion photographer? I'm trying to locate if there was a point at which the way those images came back wouldn't have worked for you—or would you have stuck to the script in any event?

Well, Adam could have taken no photographs, right? He could have declined participating, or he could have had me pay for his vacation with Meghan to the country only to come back empty handed. That wouldn't have worked for my purposes. But it's also likely that he recognized not only how the invitation opened him up to vulnerability, but also certain positive possibilities within it; for instance, that participation in the project might afford him new associations and reception contexts for his images, even some professional visibility.

And in terms of Meghan's potential for agency, is she not acting in a very constrained or narrow space? I mean, she's still the exceptional-woman image being photographed. We don't see her speaking or reading or doing things that are only for herself and not for another or for the camera.

Well . . . what might an image of her enjoying herself both be and present, besides another façade?

Okay, I see. Are you also saying I shouldn't be so sure that this can be seen, that you don't want to talk in terms of things that feel like essences? Well, that approach has been an important line of feminist discourse on self-expression and agency, against constructivist notions of the subject as performed and so on—the experiential and lived as counter to the symbolic.

Confronting Meghan with this conscious construction of tension can be perceived as, I don't want to say cruelty, but perhaps insensitivity. But I want to stress that, for me, art is about posing questions. The point is to problematize, to slow things way down, and to actually confront everyone involved with the construction of Meghan as an image, and what this means, but also to explore the cultural conditions under which these asymmetries are normalized. It's not about subjugating Meghan, but about expanding what we recognize as reality, about posing this complexity and the need for nuanced forms of reading—what Roland Barthes in *The Neutral* suggests is the overriding role of literature.

One thing that's important: in the photographs where I'm intentionally putting pressure on Meghan, she's often not looking into the camera. This tension heightens the self-consciousness around that act of photographing, whether this has to do with our personal relations or ones that are more broadly cultural. It's a blockage, a block, that's occurring. Meghan's covering herself or she's looking away, but she's there, present and also presenting herself resisting. Again, asserting the boundaries.

So do we want to distinguish between a normative photography that would objectify, and this use of the medium that is self-consciously making an object out of Meghan to repeat or replicate these dynamics?

What is really at stake here is a framing of framing. In effect, not only Meghan, but each of us is objectified in the sense that we're all lending ourselves to be used, we're all subjected to this abstract model. We are its objects. We're using ourselves, confusing that relationship between the performative and the real, but at the same time we're also bracketing these dynamics, framing a reflexive relationship to them and handing that back to the viewer.

This dynamic may produce a negative affect. One that is accentuated by the problems of authorship the piece presents, and by the unacceptable or unutterable aspect of how *Double Bind* departs from a failed marriage.

To repeat or retrace the marriage, your and Meghan's, within the marriage of Meghan and Adam, within the performing and shooting structure of *Double Bind*, this seems to me to be a concrete example of enactment. The complicity, implication, and self-implication that is demanded in enactment is something quite apart from the distance presumed by critical models in art. It's a turn against assuredness.

> I also want to underscore that while enactment sets out to double already existing structures, its meaning hinges on difference—not obvious differences, but difference at the scale of these nuanced distinctions and ways we attune ourselves to circumstances, this micropositioning that opens onto contingency and narrative, taking this up with a hyperawareness.

I suppose the shared location and the sheer number of images that were produced during each trip also helped to connect these two groups of photographs, to let not only potential connections and typologies emerge, but also distinctions.

> Definitely. There are obvious similarities overall, starting with the formal features and all the repetitions that are put in place around the photographic acts, and yet this comparative structure insists on these pronounced differences. At the same time, this is a difference that recognizes in parallel just how similarly complicit we all are, and how we can't help but be complicit.

I understand that anyone's actual sexual practice, and the symbolizations or stereotypes that might circulate for such a subject, can be very far from one another. I also remind myself that it's useful to see these images with an eye for the heterogeneity of types of desire, to be able to capture for a moment how deeply heterosexist they can seem, even if they can seem routine; even if we routinize ourselves to this imagery, take pleasure from it, etc. To be honest, I wasn't dealing with it very well as we were conceiving and taking notes for this dialogue, until we read Samuel Delany's

"Aversion/Perversion/Diversion," with its incredible respect
for narrating sexual encounters and its clarity on how socially
unrepresentable the sexual experience is in language.[4] Delany
reminds us that what is represented instead is morality about it,
forms of prohibition of it, conventionalized vantages—absences
and codings.

> It's interesting—that gap you're talking about carries implications.
> What does it mean to speak back into it, understanding that that
> unrepresentable quality is regulated through the social, that there's
> a punitive dimension to it? It reminds me of what Foucault says
> about how the exposure of sexuality serves as a means to ensure its
> concealment.

What are the limits to the performative that we've been discussing?

I can test out an idea: perhaps this is not the routine move of
deconstructing what has been made to appear as natural, and the
related critiques that are so prevalent. Affect, its ambiguity, is a real
and substantial part of this departure from such critical habits. You
assert this through the work. This is part of your position, to point
to this. There are limits placed on the structural; it's encountered
within textured conditions.

> I'm conjuring those responses, but also doing this in order to
> complicate them, for the reason that one can't reduce everything
> that's occurring in terms of the piece's internal complexity to
> that structural reading. There are these excesses that counter the
> representational cues, stating meaning only to pivot and
> reframe it.

> The thing is, these constellations of signification keep shifting,
> and the transference that this multiplicity of perspectives opens
> onto, it allows each speculation to be complicated by another
> possible perspective. Rather than desensitizing, this repetition and
> revision shifts toward an abundance of meanings—and in that, it's
> destabilizing. I am thinking about how this open-ended quality
> also doubles as an abyss of meaning.

But not creating a passive or fixed positionality for the viewer is one pointed difference here from deconstructive analysis.

> There's an ethics in acknowledging this complicity as a social fact, and there's a role that empathy plays in this. The "I" through which enactment operates extends outward toward a "you." I don't think one can stand fully outside of culture—or that one can ignore the particularities of their own subjectivity, or ignore difference or the existence of other positions and subjects—and usefully comment upon culture in any way that's not self-interested. Politically, this is the danger of receiving things from within that sheltered space of privilege, cut off from difference and disagreement, cut off from engagement.

> By articulating all these possible subject positions, and allowing us the idea that we have escape, the media actually tempers the real violence that underlies its imagery, leading us to believe that we have endless choice, that if one thing gets muddled there's always something else out there for us. Contrary to this, enactment in *Double Bind* actually shows how subjectively, but collectively as well, we share responsibility—how the subjective and social are intertwined, and there's an ethical dimension to that. Enactment arrives at this through the actual terms of our self-reflective confrontation and interaction with the other. This is what I mean about doing the very thing that I'm criticizing doing. The kind of self-reflection I'm talking about shares this empathy and acknowledgement of the other.

While the script can be seen to enact a specific set of cuts, ordering the work's environment through all these active decisions to frame (and to frame these sets of framings), one of the crucial things it does is that it raises these stereotypes. So the stereotypes you have, those structures that the project frames to be examined, are: the visual field around advertising and desire constructed by the media; modes of address used in photography, and in public and private representations; and mass-cultural heteronormative values. Those are the large things, and then you have this notion of the vernacular use of the photograph, how visual images circulate and how we circulate ourselves as images. This can't help but touch upon our relations to our bodies and the erotic, and even how we might use the erotic, intimacy, or desirability to reflect on the social frameworks around us.

> Contextually, this functions between two poles of meaning: the calling-out of both permissive, self-expressionistic uses of photography, and, on the other side of the spectrum, certain corrective, orthodox prohibitions on depicting the corporal—those moral positions that police the activity and meaning of certain social behavior.

> As a male subject, I'm implicated in these structures of looking and representing, desiring and being desired. I'm not saying that as a man I feel the effects of this in the same way as Meghan—even so, it's impossible for me to be exempt. I am complicit. I'm aslo positioned and exploited by these structures.

> During our reflections on *Double Bind*, it has started to dawn on me just how related this is to a larger philosophical or discursive binary, between the structural and the subjective, or, put another way, between the rational and the emotional—and it's astounding to me how gendered this binary is. There's a hierarchy that's upheld through pathologizing the emotional, excluding it, placing restraints on it, casting its eruptions as irrational and dysfunctional, even antisocial or destructive, and relocating it to a space without language, that can't be spoken; a space of lack.

That's part of what we're pinpointing when we discuss this notion of the gap, isn't it?

> Well it strikes me how this structural ordering is always given masculine or rational attributes, but those feminine qualities, those excesses, can disrupt, and can be used tactically to draw out those structural asymmetries, the same as those racial positions of lack which Fred Moten discusses particularly well in his writings on Adrian Piper's interventions. Enactment is about straddling these positions, and putting them into play against each other

in order to reveal how existing structures functionalize the meaning, reading, and categorization of these positions in order to uphold their own self-interests as truth. The social regulates these hierarchies through carefully framing the modes through which we understand them: through inclusions and exclusions, or through visibilities and invisibilities.

It's not one simple structure we're talking about then, is it? Enactment has a doubling. What is the source of the work's title, *Double Bind*?

> *Double Bind*, the title I gave the project, is a reference to Bateson's theorization of schizophrenia, which he later extended to theorize the importance of intertextuality in relation to creativity and problem solving. To have a double bind, basically, you have to have a primary injunction that comes with a real and severe consequence, contradicted directly by a secondary injunction that might be happening on a higher order of meaning. One message, a verbal message, for instance, might be directly contradicted by body language—

The primary injunction would be something articulated, and the secondary would come along with it.

> Two distinct, incompatible registers must be mapped over each other. For the subject to be placed in a double bind, both injunctions have to be in direct conflict with each other, and carry a threat to the subject. Confronting these messages angled against each other, the individual finds herself thrown into a "damned if I do, damned if I don't" scenario. A double bind is a position that is contradictory, that can't be resolved.
>
> In this sense, it's very similar to Melanie Klein's notions around the good breast/bad breast. In Klein's conception, at a certain point in development the infant comes to realize these paradoxical qualities of the mother's breast, how it's both nourishing and withholding. These coexisting properties within the same object are experienced as a split in the object, which manifests a parallel

split in the subject. Due to the child's absolute dependence, this is experienced as a threat, which leads to what Klein terms the depressive position, from which the child has to figure out ways to constructively come to terms with these contradictions. Applied learning, and individualizing one's own thoughts, forming opinions and positions, stem from this. These contradictions function in a catalytic way; they activate.

Are we left with the notion of elective negation and refusal tactics, to split off from the collective?

Well, in a later elaboration on double binds, Bateson spoke of an interruption into the coherence of a given context, so that learning about learning gets called into question. The mixed messages make it so the subject is not sure which context is correct or incorrect. In fact, there's no correct context, and this is experienced as an emotional disturbance. At the same time, the double bind asserts that all meaning is utterly dependent on context. Culture is chock full of these intertextual contradictions that can be deeply conflicting to the individual subject, but perhaps most importantly in this split between the structural and the subjective, cultural and psychological—however you want to put it. The tendencies for consensus, or unquestioned group unanimity, are simply other forms of patterning that should be looked at. Negation poses contradiction so it can be examined.

The contradictory space of culture and psyche, collective and individual/family . . . That resonates with the long-term work you did before *Double Bind*. You mentioned previously how *Double Bind* might present a working-through of the contradictions of *Pretend You're Actually Alive*. Do both *Pretend* and *Double Bind* produce a provoking confrontation, a catalytic negotiation of contradiction? How do they differ in doing so?

Overall, I would agree they do. But I'd add that, in contrast to how *Double Bind*'s address emphasizes the relational, *Pretend*—made over an eight-year period, but actually extending back in time much further—takes a long-term, diachronic viewpoint.

Even though the sequence and the installation of the work were anything but linear, its duration referenced models of narrative that we tend to associate with biography. There were these long-term developments in *Pretend*, so we saw the coexistence of former selves set alongside those momentary projections on her part, these kinds of extreme struggles over identifying with or negating all these external expectations being placed on her. My entrance point was through a kind of empathy and identification with my mother, where I was helping her to actualize some aspect of herself, a kind of counter or negation to the context she was situated in. Distinct from this, in *Double Bind* my self-objectification may have been aimed back at judgment structures within reception, certain tendencies that came up around *Pretend*, through embodying a copy or analog of her role. Both projects resonate with each other in how they position myself, as well as the viewer, in the middle of that crisis, implicating us in turn, so that these same instances of projected fantasies and identifications are present, all highlighted. In *Double Bind*, though, by framing this multiplicity of images, this mass of fragmentary moments, within a compact period of time, the shooting acts trace and record the cognitive space of the photographic interaction. Rather than emphasize biography to the same excruciating degree as in the atmosphere with my mother in *Pretend*, because of its shifted relation to authorship *Double Bind* emphasizes the present moment of the situation. The scope of both still constitute systems.

Is there a distinction here that has to do with genre or vernacular photography or realism? Is that what's so crucial about some of these differences in address?

The reception of that work with my mother was particularly difficult to manage for me: some viewers' and writers' seeming need to judge felt so deep-seated that it threatened to override even basic looking. There was one tendency to sensationalize the work as taboo, reducing it to this absurd Oedipal reading, as though it was some narrow chronicle of an erotic relationship between my mother and me. This misrecognized as fact aspects of our relationship that in reality were highly ambiguous, while it ignored how my mother was using her sexuality to negotiate complex social dynamics, both from the standpoint of power within the family, but also power that was gendered and economic on a broader social level. This also refused to recognize how she was performing a self-objectification as a negation, as a means of directing affect to destabilize and problematize a set of assumed social truths. I started wondering whether the main charge may have been located not in my mother's sexuality but in my tolerance toward that part of her life, the very fact that I wasn't turning away from it—that I was even enabling her to fulfill something that people might regard in light of a narrow morality. Staging it this way—without saying it means this or that—interferes with viewers' desires to categorize.

In terms of this tradition of photographing from experience—of photographing partners and family members, having to do with both that tradition's claims to authenticity and its liberalized, highly conventionalized, transgressive vernacular—I was ambivalent. I was ambivalent then, especially concerning aspects of my mother's own desires to be photographed, and on a more general level I still am, because of the genre's individualism, values, and judgments, all its means of externalizing and dissociating.

Double Bind differs from this in terms of how it casts participation: for instance, Meghan's and Adam's complicity, and the distinct intersubjective conditions encountered by the three of us performing from lived experience, this also takes shape under these contractual terms, and within these limited durations, and with the camera cast as feedback.

Perhaps it's a more subtle, sideways movement in *Pretend*, how the authorization of speaking from the autobiographical is undermined by means of your speaking with your mother, and by the techniques of speaking from an implicated and crossed position (crossed in terms of identification and gender) from inside the performing of your mother's sexualized world view?

There's something very productive and demanding about this messiness. I've always gravitated toward works that demand this,

where as a viewer I'm forced to reorient. Experiencing the work
with any depth means taking it up as a lens, and individuating a
relationship to it. The archetypes prop up an identification and I'm
using them in specific ways to short-circuit the tendency for people
to symptomatize singular subjects, rather than culture at large. This
tactic aims to create a constructive social criticism from within, by
taking on the terms of the culture and its contradictions, and by
really asking what the materials of the work reveal about culture at
large. There is an ethics embedded in this type of looking, and one
that is not utopic.

I think your work puts forward a technique for the artist to show—
that is, to copresent and make visible—the expression of others
that is relational, and promising for how this is done without the
presumed privilege based upon authorized speaking, as we know it
in criticism. By that I mean the usual relations of who is authorized
to speak and who they elect to speak about. Your techniques are
self-objectifying, self-implicating, and performed with these subjects
who are participants (and not essentialized subjects). In this way, I
see you working outside objectification as it typically takes place
within representation.

For me, as a creator of this dialogue, executed in relation to your
work and with you, my techniques similarly shift away from
objectification and the usual authorizations that come with being a
scholar, a critic.

4.   Samuel Delany, "Aversion/Perversion/Diversion,"
in *Longer Views: Extended Essays* (Hanover and London:
Wesleyan University Press, 1996), 119–143.

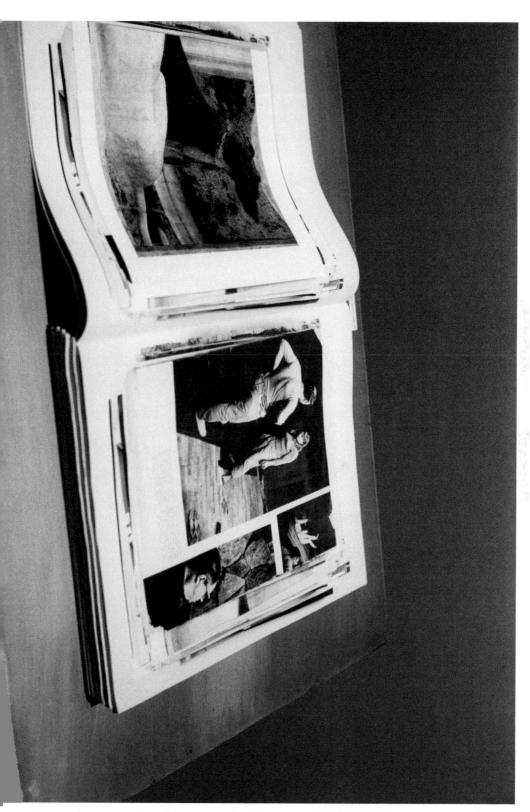

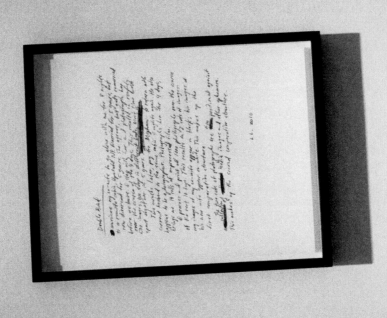

Double Bind

~~I~~ convince my ex-wife to go alone with me for 3 nights
to a remote cabin, Upstate NY. Married for 5 years, but
now divorced for 5 years. She agrees, but gets remarried
before we leave. I stay with her and photograph her
over the course of the 4 days. This results in roughly
500 images. We sleep in different ~~beds~~. Most time we've
spent together in 5 years. ~~~~

Two months later, pay for Meghan to return with
current husband to the same cabin 3 nights again. He also
happens to be a photographer. Photographs her for 4 days,
brings me 14 rolls of unprocessed film.

I process and print all 1000 photographs over the course
of the next 10 days. This results in 2 sets of images:
my images of my ex-wife appear on black; his images of
his new wife appear on white. This makes up the
first comparative structure.

The two sets of photographs are ~~they~~ positioned against
a ~~collection of~~ ~~found~~ media images and other ephemera.
This makes up the second comparative structure.

L.L. 2010

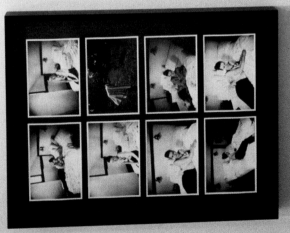

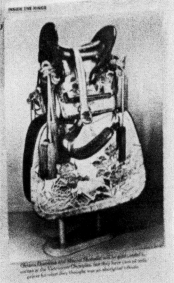

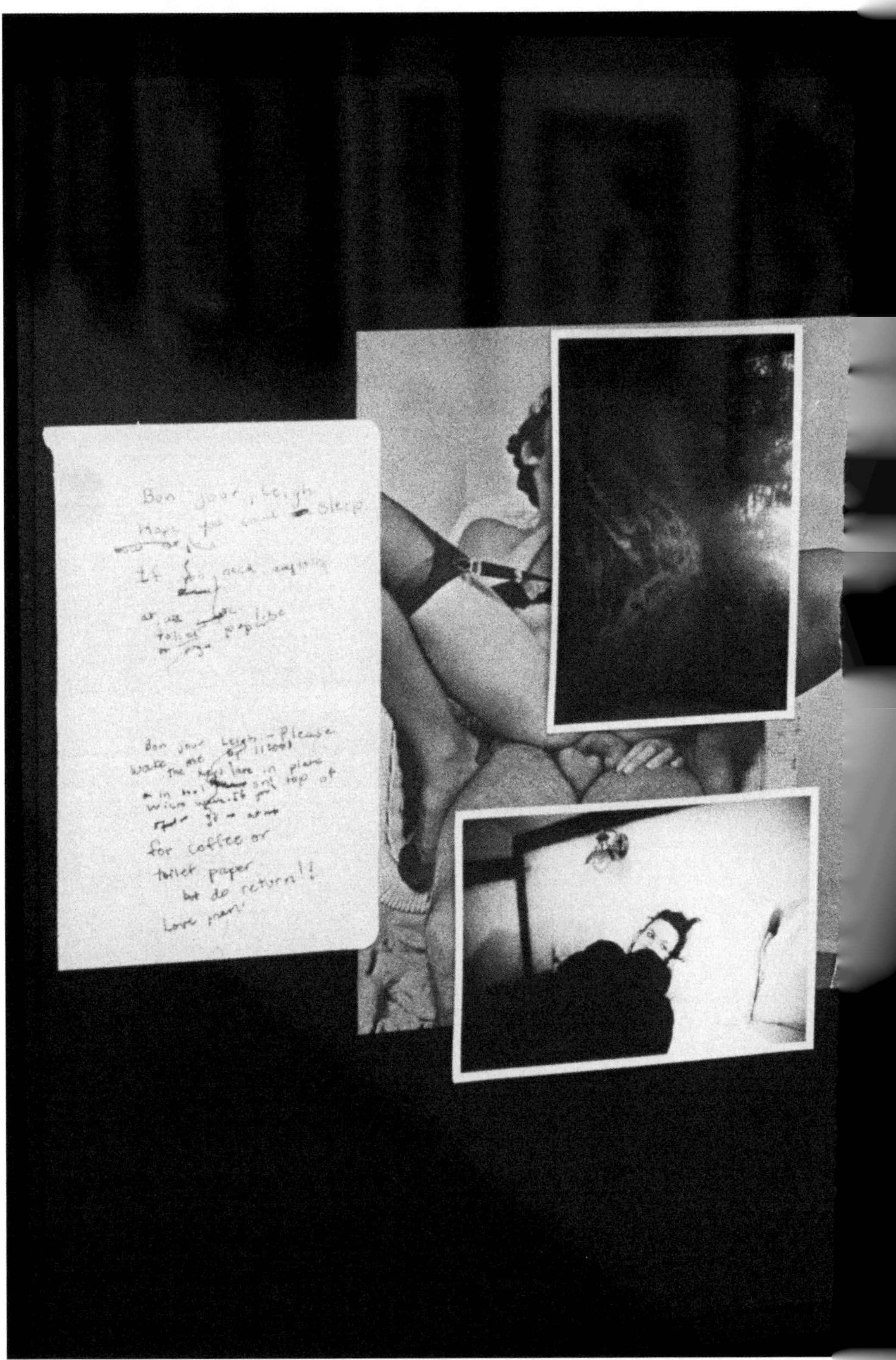
Bon jour, Leigh
for coffee or
toilet paper
but do return!!
Love marie

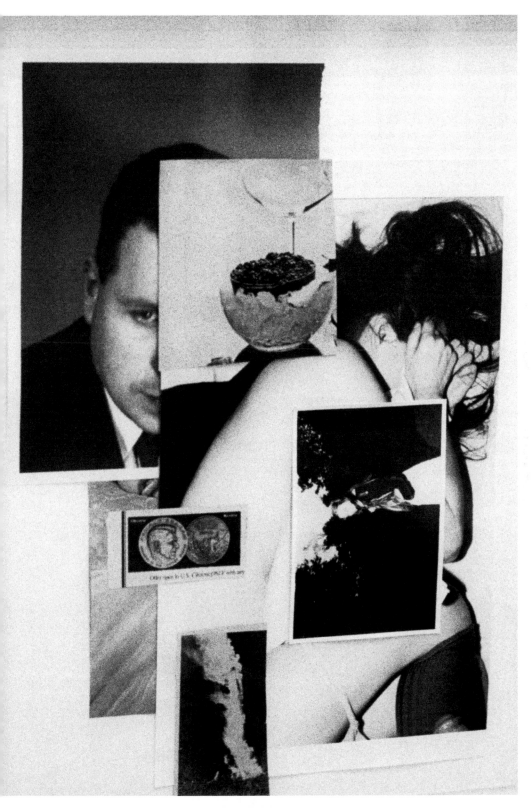

Thomas Bernhard in Ohlsdorf, 1981

Thomas Bernhard und Hedwig Stavianicek in Ohlsdorf

Indian scouts, along with an interpreter and an officer, crouch for battle in Arizona's desert country, where a 24 year campaign taught the Army the truth of the proverb "Only an Apache can catch an Apache."

118

5. Dialogue, *continued*

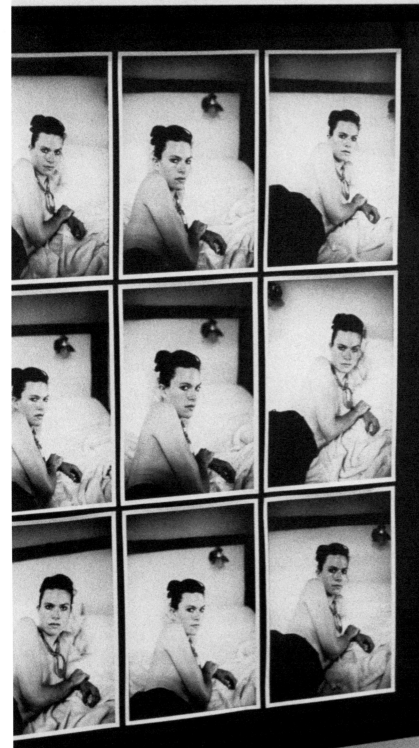

LEIGH LEDARE : I think it's important to consider the form of *Double Bind*'s installation, as well as the presence of the work in physical space. At The Box in Los Angeles, a rather large, freestanding room was built to house the piece, inside the gallery's main space. The outside of that room was made up of raw plywood, and the walls created a boundary between its exterior and interior space, themselves functioning as a kind of container—not unlike the script—separating the piece from what was happening around it inside the larger gallery. This situated it as a singular object: a room built within a room that comprised a kind of system. The viewer entered through one of two doorways, positioned asymmetrically on either side of the room.

In New York, at Mitchell-Innes & Nash, this relationship between outside and inside was constructed differently. Walls were built that partitioned one very large space into three separate rooms. Two smaller rectangular galleries led, one after the other, back to a larger square gallery at the rear of the space. The viewer first entered into a room with the project *An Invitation*.[5] Through a doorway cut into one wall, the viewer then accessed a second room, which functioned as a simplified diagram of *Double Bind*.

RHEA ANASTAS : This first of two rooms for *Double Bind* contained three elements: a steel table, on top of which sat a stack of the six magazines of the *Ephemera* publication which, without a vitrine or plexi top, the viewer was free to leaf through.[6] Then, installed tightly facing one another on either side of one of the room's corners, were two panels, one with a black background and one with a white one, a visual statement of *Double Bind*'s basic diptych structure. Finally, the project description was placed beside the entranceway leading into the largest of the interior rooms with *Double Bind*: the grouping of photographs, panels, vitrines.

The project description has been placed differently over the various installations. In this case, the emphasis was on encountering it first, just outside the entry to the large interior room.

The description, with its script for the performances, gained something from a proximity to the media collection of the *Ephemera* magazines. The elements were held in a highly contrasting relationship. This lent a layered quality to the media element of the work, just the fact of being able to view the media materials in the vitrine in the larger interior room (amongst the work's other photography and montages) against the periodical pages that can be viewed up close in the emptier room.

> How would you characterize some of the differences between this emptier "diagram" room and the room that followed, the interior room?

The initial effect was also almost like walking into an installation view of the piece, but in space. I recall thinking about the two framed panels that were hanging—I think one had an image that was close to a still life—and puzzling over whether the imagery itself had some initial message to convey: you know, why these two, of all forty-eight?

> It took me quite a long time to select the panels, though I knew that I wanted this diptych to be the first or among the first objects to be caught in the viewer's sight line. The play of the horizontal table on which the magazines were placed and these vertical framed elements interested me. It was important to set the project description apart from the amassing of *Double Bind*, similar to the arrangement at The Box.

The framed panels that I initially encountered upon entering the main room set my attention on this black-and-white framing code that designates whether the photographs on each panel are yours or Adam's, and sets these up dialectically. If I followed a linear walk-through, the diptychs came on stronger and stronger, one after the other, starting first with the images from the two trips alone, set against each other, before the scope and heterogeneity gained in intensity, with more and more of the mass-cultural materials being mixed in.

> Yes. The works were hung low and wrapped around the whole

of the interior. This compressed the installation, spreading it out horizontally. Included were all the various panels that contain arrangements from both collections of material—but it's not like there was a single taxonomy or one organizational approach. The grid was introduced, but the work continuously pushed against this form, referencing its logic in order to create friction against it, to disorder it in various ways. This disordering echoed how the piece works with photography and all the issues that come along with the authority of that ocular perspective.

In the three vitrines that stood in the center of the space I could observe the components and different groups of materials that are seen together in the installations. Focusing on the three vitrines within the room's interior, each one isolated out its own order of imagery. Two smaller vitrines, one black and one white, contained all the remaining photographs from your trip and Adam's, respectively, that weren't worked into the diptychs. In these vitrines the singular photographs were arranged in stacks which, because of the paper, had curled or curved edges—like your grids, there was hardly rectitude or rigidity. These stacks drew a visual relationship to the piles of mass-media materials that were included in a larger vitrine, one of which was nearly brimming with found pages. I could hold these materials as separate, even though in the diptychs this was countered by the composing or layouts, with distinct orders of imagery permeating and fading into each other.

Still, you were left with the way that each vitrine situated these materials as a collection or large-scale amassing, systematizing them, each distilled as specific sets of relations. So, as much as being presented with content, each vitrine confronted you with a distinct logic or circuit of address . . . On a very simple level: wife/husband (and viewer), ex-wife/ex-husband (and viewer), or media imagery (photography as apparatus)/viewer.

Was this to set up the assumption of some act of mapping, where each served as an allegory for the other? It's as if to say that everyone was simultaneously implicated in the positions of subject, object, producer, and viewer.

Each of the vitrines also had a distinct tone. Let's take the media collection. One encountered it on its own in a vitrine, in a very physical way as this heap of torn pages: multiple images, or single images on a page, without any binding from the original magazines or newspapers. This was a wave of imagery, almost a tour of the history of color printing. Traces of context were there, a lot of them identifiable—obviously, because you hadn't clipped. For these you tore out full sheets and retained the printed page as a whole unit, but counter to this there were many moments in the montages where these magazine pages had been arranged with a small amount of clipping or cutting.

What happens when the tones of irony (in advertising or editorial content) and promotion or bombastic celebration (fashion imagery, paparazzi shots of actors and starlets)—qualities that appear in the media imagery, which also includes a whole range of images with off-color humor, erotic play, misogyny—are made to interact with the private images' loaded, serious, and often somber quality (which we can sense but also project from the script), and with their more quotidian expressions of anticipation, fulfillment, distance, or disappointment?

Even after all this time, it's hard to fully wrap myself around the volume of printed materials and the heterogeneity of looks and impressions or moods that accompany them. This volume of printed material, it's also more than can be made visibly accessible in the process of being organized physically in the vitrines.

And the act of reading the work can't be separated from a reading of the specific tones and colors of these examples: for instance, a magazine page depicting a couple participating in scream-therapy sessions at the Esalen Institute in the late sixties; or another magazine page, where the proverb "Only an Apache can catch an Apache" captions a printed group photograph of Native American scouts who have been paid off by the American army to participate in the genocide of their own tribe. Here, it feels that humor is being used to cast complicity as a game, and the ease of this trickiness appears to me as excessively brutal. If nothing else, this incident is being relegated to a historical story, but also made comic and undermining, and not seen as systemic still.

Counter to this, there are pages pulled out of reporting on significant political events. Or there may be a quieter cultural page, at home with an intellectual.

Maybe it's satire versus glimpses into historically specific moments . . .

These encapsulations are so potent, something at the same time very heavy-handed and full of a satirical humor that feels dangerous, sliding everywhere. The *Ephemera* magazines, which take these tear sheets and recompose them into six printed magazines, seem to set up an oppositional structure in order to deal very directly with the tones the images carry. I am thinking of juxtapositions such as the ads for breast augmentation surgery that appear suddenly beside a sales pitch for the antidepressant Paxil; or a page from coverage of Timothy Leary traveling with Eldridge Cleaver in Algeria, paired with a treatment of a black journalist's problems reporting for the white media; or Max Ernst shown with his Hopi kachina collection coupled with Harlem adolescents pictured on a visit to the king of Sweden, in his throne room.

As you say, how do these images play with the private photographs? There's a satirical resonance between them. Also, set-off by the images of the two trips for *Double Bind*, contextual overlays such as these in the media, that euphemize, are seen to be underwritten by real relations and asymmetries.

It follows then that violence may be necessary to address. Feminist interventions are also pitched toward this violence and are themselves violent, to raise antagonisms rather than accept a subordinate position toward these antagonisms. In one way, the structural analyses of feminist critiques cut into the humor, exposed its dynamics and assumptions. But certain meanings were emphasized over others, and asymmetries of power were for the most part the targeted relationship.

There's a page from *Life* magazine that's an ad for an advertising firm, juxtaposed with a page that refers to how Hitler amassed a private fortune by collecting royalties off his appearance on the German postal system's stamps—talk about a shift from asymmetry of power into a subtler form of expropriation! And there's a review of Simone de Beauvoir's *The Coming of Age*.

One that sticks with me is a mid-2000s reference to Wilde's *Dorian Grey*, made by a teen clothing company, a Mexican company. What does it mean to hold this advertisement in mind with the serial imagery of Meghan?

Earlier we mentioned how the images of Meghan have this iconic quality and are echoed cross-reflectively against equivalent icons in the media. But there are also all these other leitmotifs that counterpoint around the installation—distinctions within how Meghan may be pictured by Adam or myself, or how the contexts against which similar images of Meghan appear may radically shift the meanings of those images. The image of Meghan is continually present and has the effect of surrounding the viewer. It sets an emotional tone, something almost filmic, immersing the viewer in her looking and the looking that surrounds her image. That confrontation is also a kind of conscience.

I do and don't see what you mean by *conscience* . . . Yes, she stands as an individual, a bastion of privacy and interiority against the mass-cultural pages. But still, because of the suggestiveness, provocativeness of the triangle of crossed relationships, and given the three positions and also the viewer's, it's hard to say whose conscience about doing what to whom is represented, if you know what I mean.

Sure, but it's also necessary to take what any actor expresses as a source of motivation to be on one level real, as constitutive of real motivations, and to recognize the validity of these multiple viewpoints rather than force a structure over them. That's another reason to withdraw from thatsubjective/objective division.

There are also all these nuances of positioning that can be located
in the media addresses: more hostile forms of advertising, for
one, may have emerged irreverently as a counter to advertising's
attempts to sell people things they didn't need. Same for off-color
political commentary that pointed out how deeply fractured race
and gender relations had become, despite state-level rhetoric that
attempted to focus attention away from these domestic issues and
onto the Cold War or Vietnam instead. Also, depictions of male
figures as clowns or buffoons may have spoken to how emasculated
people felt inside these conditions, against which depictions of
female nudes within men's magazines were perhaps the flip side,
creating an image of an idealized salve.

I thought for a moment that you said slave. That image or fantasy
applies to the nudes, too.

And while it was a way of countering what at that time was a
scripting of morality that increasingly rang false, it may have been
forwarding certain interests at the expense of others. There were
obvious destructive byproducts, which is core to the critiques
feminism has made.

Well, *Double Bind*'s insistence on the triangle, on overlaps and
interrelationships . . . It seems to me that this complicates the
sometimes monolithic way that these critiques located addresses
and objectifications.

There's also a crossing of contexts, one stemming out of more
avant-garde or edgy traditions of satire such as Lenny Bruce, Joseph
Heller, and Terry Southern, which later got incorporated into
advertising and popularized as madcap humor by someone like Stan
Freberg, who appealed to the dissonant strains of counterculture. It
strikes me that a dark sense of absurdity was the prerequisite for
these forms of irony. And this use of gallows humor or irreverence
poses an oppositional force: the counterculture's tactics to outwit
the state or institution, or morality. Of course, eventually these
things get institutionalized, in turn, or desublimated, and their
original meanings fall off, intentions shift or falter.

It sounds to me that you're trying to consider these images less as representations than as phenomena or evidence, windows onto specific social dynamics. So what does it mean to insist on the importance of those moments and to draw them forward, with the insistence on the specificity of the enacted situations, into the moment of 2010?

The more important question is, where does this cultural humor become an end in itself, a kind of apparatus, a shield or distancing device, as opposed to being used to get at something deeper? Or when do things become so deeply fucked up that apathy sets in fully? This is something which social media may also symptomatize.

I think at the time of making *Double Bind*, I was working though this crisis of meaning, responding to it in a way that was attempting to reinvest it all with something subjective that felt extremely important. Maybe the digital is tied into this, but I think on the basis of this apathy that underlies our moment, our social and political conditions: this whole sense of how we no longer know what institutions or ideas to place our trust in.

Do we need to look at humor as a specific mode of affect, cultural affect? It plays out consistently for a while, then something shifts and its effect is suddenly something else, in the same way an old affect might become fatigued . . .

The Internet, for one, seemed to represent a shift out of the limitations of a politically correct cultural moment, but it still maintains certain things. For instance, by enabling pornography to circulate privately, it takes pressure off what might formerly have been seen as a hypocritical pleasure. While it facilitates a wider presence, slightly less hidden or closeted, for sexuality, it's a maybe strangely nonsocial version of sexuality, sanitized, stripped of contexts, and disconnected from interrelational responsibilities individuals have to each other via the distance and mediation of the digital.

I can appreciate perversity, or mischief, or even play for that matter, but it seems unfulfilling as an end in and of itself, without also containing some active capacity for reflection.

Mischief with serious purpose? *Double Bind* strikes me as full of sadness, pathos.

I agree. But it also takes what pleasures it can in its humorous moments, and these things are nested inside each other.

We also need to look at social typing: how these stock characters that occupy the media images are archetypes, players within the anthropological and cultural stories that we pass down and draw from to explain the world to ourselves. Lévi-Strauss's anthropology is one example—and *Double Bind* may bring to mind the exchange of women as a social contract in patriarchy—and then there's also the tabloids, not to mention the narratives that accompany reality television, with their revanchist roles (the bachelor, the millionaire, the criminal). These roles may actually have a lot to say about our depictions of class and social conflict, what we feel threatened by, our vicarious identifications, or even our needs to other.

Take the role of the trickster: duplicity might actually be valued, openly accepted or tolerated in one instance of culture, by one viewpoint, but not by another. There might be an underdog identification, one that subverts through certain forms of indirection that are open to it. Michael Taussig has distinguished these tactics from more colonizing forms of control, what he refers to as the "dissimulation of dissimulation," the constructed appearance of rationalism and authority which functions to police, but which also serves as a blind for more systematic types of deception, ones regulated through bureaucracy.

The figure of the artist is another myth . . .

There's a kind of cultural absurdity in this, a low-level brutality, and sadness, that's not reading clearly. I don't have a handle on it, not by a long shot. I sometimes think it might be conceptualized through an editorial principle, the how of the selecting. Was it narrative and juxtapositions that drove you to pull out one story, then another? Was it the resonance a given page would have when held up to the black and whites, to the stories of you and Meghan and you and Adam?

> I think it's something deeper. Humor, but also tragedy, play necessary functions as cultural release valves, cutting through pretense to reveal this morass of conflicts and contradictions that underwrite the social. This itself constitutes a kind of theater, a spectacle of cruelty, and that's something we're complicit in—and something I'm interested in. I'm not suggesting these materials are implicitly critical though—they have to be framed as such, framed to open up reflection. We have to actively assert our relationship to them, rather than passively adopt them as spectacle. Nor can we pretend these cruel and complicated contradictions don't exist.

Yes, there may be something to this idea of yours. Restated, it's something like, we have to find ways to make complicated again the potential for taking in spectacle in serious, contrary ways, to open up our ability to reflect on how we actually engage with spectacle and visibility, and, I should say, social typing—with all of this.

How did you begin collecting the print media?

> I regularly collect things, so initially it was just business as usual. Then there were a few key places I would visit looking for materials: used bookstores, garage sales, swap meets. I found that in Los Angeles, where I was living at the time, in 2009–2010, there was all this cultural detritus. Unlike New York, where everyone lives in apartments, having more space, people in LA tend to save things. This meant that magazines and other printed objects hadn't been thrown away and that it was still possible to find these materials. I also purchased some magazines online, and when I would travel for other projects, say to Moscow, Turin, or Berlin, I would use this as an excuse to collect more. We should also mention that I incorporated things other than media materials in the collection of ephemera, too, things I'd been saving

for some time: personal artifacts, found photographs, various notes and fliers, drawings, my and Meghan's marriage certificate, photographs that Larry Clark had taken of me, to name a few.

Were there magazines or periodicals that you were following? Did you have a certain understanding of editorial processes or styles, or of one social and political moment over another—or did you find that as you started gathering things?

I always try to take my cues from listening closely to my materials, which in this case were quite vast. But this process starts intuitively, with me not always knowing why I'm looking at something, and if that looking continues, it usually means something is there. The other thing is that in looking at this volume of imagery, once you're familiarized with the material, you start seeing through the initial representations. You get to a place where you start seeing things differently—noticing, for instance, how crucial these broader affects are . . .

So I found myself looking for certain attitudes or personalities that the images were conveying, how they seemed to be pointing beyond themselves as representations, to various ideologies they were expressing, and also to impulses that weren't so consciously focused. Images are traces of actions and situations, and in that they can be configured to pose models of relationality, something akin to Benjamin's dialectics of seeing.

I am thinking about the potential or possibility of the mass-cultural materials of *Double Bind*, how they may recast the genre of realism that *Pretend* locates, even if it is a mediated or self-aware use of realism—the realism, in other words, of a highly mediated reality. A low-level burn of brutality infuses the materials of *Double Bind*. What may first look like huge contrasts between the personal photographs from the trips and the media materials then possibly start to look like smaller differences. I'm not sure . . . this moves back and forth, it doesn't stay stable, for me anyway. The comparative structure itself casts the work's relationships as a high form of theater.

With *Pretend*, the fictionalization of identity—your mother's performance—was about using affect and the corporeal to destabilize, and about playing, entertaining, also considering or reflecting, seeing herself, and hustling . . .

> Yeah, but it was also about calling forward and complicating the judgments of other people, and there was something so devastatingly ungrounded in this, in the way that all these different positions she was occupying and identifying with were ultimately irreconcilable. There is also the question of how I'm cast in relation to my mother, the question of how she may be victimizing me— always some viewers wish to project this onto me. I've certainly played with assumptions like these. . . complicated them, as well as exploited them.

> But doesn't this speak to broader situations of cultural scripting and of ways we might play with this. It's almost like realism recast through the media as "lifelike." I have to take into account too the brutality of letting someone hollow themselves out in front of the camera, that kind of Artaudian cruelty. This could also be seen as a testing or questioning of value. How does this operate within my playing with this volume of mass-cultural materials? Does my collecting all the crass material, and placing it there, constitute another hollowing out? If we aren't able to invest in the apparatus of this material in a positivistic way, then what exactly is it that we're left with? It makes me think of libertinism, or this obsession with the *jeune fille*.

It's confusing. The crassness you mention of the found media materials sets off the beauty and desirability of Meghan in a surprising way. Does it diminish this desirability? Does it make it more real, more intimate, or more tender? What does it do, beyond simply revealing how susceptible we are to being manipulated through the production of desire?

In some sense, I'm that viewer who has the tendency to keep that line between the privacy-made-public of the photographs of Meghan and the visual pathology of the mass-cultural imagery fairly

distinct, in order to focus on how identity looks, how it's formed,
thinking that there might be an interiority that moves against the
violence of the cultural. Libertinism would perhaps be located
here, more on the side of the doer and autonomy. Is the aesthetic,
is this separation, a cut from the collective as well? I think the
work asks this question, even if the mixed panels and comparative
structure also push a systemic reading, regarding the social typing of
capitalism. It's hard for me to see the *jeune fille* as a strong negative
or anticapitalist idea, since it has its female social typing: it is a
Euroethno-economic type of youth, whiteness, social class, etc.

> What is it to act against the sterility of culture and the politically
> correct? The point of the subjective may be a counter to this
> hollowing out and giving over, a way of insisting on some
> sentiment that is vital, that isn't sanitized or degraded but is simply
> about engagement. In spite of this cultural cynicism, there's
> an earnestness.

I can say, provisionally, there was a cultural context in the
early and mid-2000s in which irony reigned, along with a
postfeminist thinking that was distanced from any kind of
image or writing, a vantage that would make the mass-cultural
materials seem like no big deal, and would be equally indifferent
to the relationship triangle of you/Meghan/Adam, and to the
photographing and sharing of these images. With this idea
in mind, I think some consideration of this cultural moment
could shed light on the private-public dynamics of *Double Bind*,
on its sensory overload, but also on its belief in the aesthetic. At
the moment of the work's conception, reality television has
emerged, so have political scandals in which private images
are outed . . .

But with irony, the questions of economic and cultural and male
privilege all come to mind. The distanced position of irony seems
immune to the visual pathology of the world. Why, I wonder—I
mean, for whom? Whose life isn't touched by these asymmetries
of power?

I feel like we have to formulate why the body is so important right now. Or maybe more precisely, why subjectivity is still so important.

Yes, absolutely. Hasn't this dialogue been consistently preoccupied by that? I feel we will be criticized for our fixation on the body, accused of creating a new essentialism, which is not what we're up to, not in the least.

Isn't it quite historically specific though? A lot of this material channels what might be thought of as containment strategies: anxieties around certain gender or political or class issues are posed in ways that are reactionary and attempting to manage. This seems rampant during specific historical moments, even if it can't be so cleanly isolated. For instance, even now we might be dealing with the residue of certain gender attitudes introduced in the seventies, which themselves were reactions to changing gender relations and the failure of the revolutionary movements that characterized the late sixties. Then there was a very conservative shift in the nineties, and now obvious differences have emerged. I found myself choosing a lot of materials that focused on issues around corporeality for the reason that the body seemed to be one of the key cultural sites where all this pressure came to bear, being used in the capacity of some sort of collective release valve.

This whole problem of the public, which in some senses feels like a problem of the private—how I try to be private, but can't be, how privacy can't be maintained . . .

There's also an idea that *Double Bind* might be reproducing what a lot of people already do on social media, but much more meticulously and self-consciously—for instance, sexting or revenge porn. Oddly enough, when these activities erupt in some kind of social scandal, like a politician outing his own infidelities, it's not so much the pornographic content that's violent but the casualness and spontaneity with which it's produced and circulated.

I think the images of *Double Bind* are constructed and pitched very differently than that kind of personal photography that we see on social media. I think it's a red herring, that comparison; it doesn't go anywhere.

> But still, it's a part of the context, even if the work pits itself against the expectations of confessional culture or the sharing of privacy on the web.

To say something else, then, in material terms: there's also this somewhat inchoate quality of the media artifacts in the work, a feeling of aging materials with fading, older print qualities, a texture and physicality that is resolutely against the digital. The photographic prints are actual silver-gelatin prints, and the media collection appears in its originally printed and distributed forms, not reproduced as lithographs or cleaned up in any way.

> I was interested in the traces of use on these materials. I was also interested in how certain events from the historical record, which I'd known only as their edited and organized versions, appeared within their initial context in this mass media, alongside all this additional information. It's straight noise: ads for ads, information about information, magazines selling back issues of other magazines . . . In compiling the collection, I tried to give a wide view to encompass both the historically important and also the trash, which seemed to speak to the experience and distractions that characterize history as it's actually occurring and being witnessed. This wide view also seemed to echo the effects of the proliferation of content online, like the unedited uploading of personal digital photographs on social-media sites (e.g., here's my vacation, my wedding photos, etc.). It's this dialogue that *Double Bind* has with the digital, as figure and ground—the digital surrounds the viewing of the piece, it forms a context.

This brings to mind taste and the question of what's included in art, through taste, and what isn't. Are you doing this considering the decorum of the contemporary, its allowable aesthetics? Think of how your and Adam's photos are set in a dualism with the supposed bad taste and misogyny of the found materials . . .

It's an interesting question, but I'd also ask, what exactly is my aesthetic? There's a look, but it's also always been about intervening in something that already exists; it's always a borrowing. That's another aspect of my work that is mercurial. In the work with my mother, for instance, it's more or less she who is the art director for the entire work.

It seems that you're also sort of making a gesture to the discourse of the archive, while at the same time using *Double Bind* as a counter to that discursive form, and the authority of a focused interest or research agenda. Could we propose that *Double Bind* is doing something different, placing together moments or cuts into history for what they can show us about the shifts in how affect has been used?

Sure, and another way that the body comes forward in *Double Bind* is through Meghan's being captured in the photographs as a signifier of beauty and youth.

I wonder what values get produced from this fixation on Meghan during her youth. Because of the ageless and timeless quality of photography, it's there to be observed and dealt with. I discern in the work an idea about—and maybe a pleasure, too—using an imagery that takes up the body, that seems to want to say that the body and the visceral level of things is very important, but that does so quite apart and outside of the cultural zeitgeist of corporeal imagery that's going on at the time, that's basically about pornography becoming mainstream.

I don't know if you can attach it to that, but the cultural body may experience a parallel aging, transformation, exhaustion, and outmoding, one where new bodies and ideas might need to emerge on the stage, rather than us trying to call forward the same old ones.

Also, we can't assume that images of sexuality are necessarily sexual, at least in a relational sense, when they might instead represent a cleaning up of the sexual, something experienced alone, something sanitized from the complication of connection. This also makes me think of an ad that is included in one diptych: an American Apparel ad with a famous porn actress, Faye Reagan. What if you just want a pair of underwear and not sex?

You're monkeying around again, in that diptych!

Well, it just strikes me as a kind of empty form of subversion . . . Apart from the wide scope of the question about the body, there's also a way in which at the time I didn't care to make singular photographs. In the early-to-mid-2000s, photography no longer seemed to be about selecting a negative from a role of film that had to then be printed. *Double Bind* acknowledges this by the fact that I use every image taken on the two trips. So there was a negative move toward photography in the work, that was in conversation with this quality of profusion that arose around digitization.

Right, in that sense you're almost looking at the black-and-white film and the contact sheets with a digital mindset, where you're dealing with this material as an entity in itself. Is that why you gave yourself the rule of making no selections from the rolls of film shot on the trips?

In large part, and it also becomes a criteria for creating a system that echoes this new volume of material we're suddenly forced to deal with. Flusser made this great counterintuitive comment: that the most redundant thing is in fact the repetition of the new. But I want to differentiate this so-called digital mindset from the affects that are tied up with it. The truth is, we don't yet know what this digital episteme is, and I think we have to look further than simply the digital to explain what we're involved in.

No, I'm making a loose analogy, to think about how your decisions with this analog material relate to an environment that is increasingly shaped by another materiality, with an emphasis on the virtual, illusionistic, interiority, etc. . . . But no, I don't know what to ascribe to the digital and what not to, nor do I agree with this binary thing that happens in photography discourse all the time: oh, this is analog, this is digital—the identities are not actually that clear.

Yeah, that assumption is tiring. In *Double Bind*, each one of those hundreds of images of Meghan reproduces the same referent: it's extremely redundant, a thousand images of Meghan. But you're right, there's something more, something counter to the way the digital levels out meaning. This collapse is in the background of the media collection, too. But I think we have to recognize that a levelling isn't the only outcome this massive volume of materials introduces. Its volume also speaks to a relentlessness and overloading, and as the viewer has to move through this, through those temporal stages and shifts in their seeing, understanding has to be given time and space to develop, which is counter to this redundancy of the new, to this revolving door of fashion. In the process of this, spectacle might actually *détourn* and become something else.

I'm thinking about why *Double Bind* is a unique piece. You seem to be putting emphasis on the physical experience of the work and the locating of space for consideration that this implies. What ideas, what deliberations did you have regarding constructing how the viewer was going to look at the work and engage the imagery?

As I said, I'm emphasizing its quality as a system, and it's through this immersion that affect is directed at the viewer. There is a solicitous quality it takes on: it asks for something. Counter to how the materials are organized in the diptychs, the vitrines foreground this nonedit.

Well, I have to say that the term *nonedit* confuses me. I mean, there's no such thing, really; there are always compositions going on. Are you speaking rather about the quality of the work being unframed, unbounded, the opposite of packaged, as in work that goes more toward spectacle?

Okay, maybe that's misleading—by *nonedit* I mean these collections become analogous to the unordered complexity of the cultural field. Without being ordered, their volume resists being read; or rather, it has to be read systematically, not singularly.

To go against this, in the diptychs there is also this logic of variation. Variation still strikes me as an extremely specific type of composing.

> Of course. The diptychs each assert a different proposition concerning the meaning of the relationships and the stereotypes or reductions taking place. This series of variations are placed in space to become a set of contradictory and complementary social possibilities. Organized as a system, this set draws a parallel with other cultural systems.

> Also, as an installation of this scale, there's a demand that it eventually be owned by an institution or public collection with space to house it, implying that the audience for the piece would be public and collective, as opposed to a singular viewer. That's very important in how the meaning of the piece comes to include its own reception.

A duality forms within how you were just speaking about *Double Bind*, in terms of the perceived and socially sanctioned practices and forces of structure. And yet, there is this other quality to the work's materiality, a tactility, which to me feels connected to its personal side. Then there are the marks of the printed magazines and journals having been used, reused, and finally discarded. This brings to mind a simple and amazing observation of Winnicott's about our fundamental desiring for being known and for being utterly private at the same time.

> The private images and relationships become lost in the balance, absorbed into the mass-media images. Likewise, the media images inflect themselves onto the private images, and as subjects we're likewise caught—interpellated in the poiesis of our social system. The script is a kind of reminder of these individual relationships and the lived private politics that lie behind public representations.

The vitrines are also repositories. It's about leftovers, about a stacking and cancelling out. There's a representational entropy that looms over the entire project and speaks back to that poiesis.

I'm also struck by that in seeing the reconstituted magazines that make up the *Ephemera* publications. The loose materials are reconfigured as new magazines, ones that allow for a dialectical reading and pointing, and which critically contextualize this media, even while repeating it to play it against itself. Again, repetition pitched back at the apparatus.

Those magazines were made by sequencing 479 pieces of ephemera, which I then placed on a copy stand in the form of a stack and photographed, each time removing the top piece from the stack. Subtracting one page at a time, you descend through the stack until finally it's completely exhausted and you're left simply with an image of the copy stand. Finally, it's another form of self- or autoportraiture—the apparatus photographing the apparatus, copying itself. For me, this is where that volume of mass-media imagery reaches its logical conclusion, circling the drain of representational and ideological fatigue.

5.   *An Invitation*, an offset lithograph and silkscreen edition
with handwritten elements, developed out of an invitation from
an anonymous private individual, a European professional
writer who was connected to high-profile media and political
realms. The commissioner initially asked Ledare if he would be
interested in making erotic portraits on commission with her at
her home, based upon her knowledge of Ledare's prior work,
especially *Pretend You're Actually Alive*. The request was for
photographs that positioned the commissioner as the subject
and would be for private use. A conversation ensued, and was
later concretized through a contract facilitated by a lawyer. The
arrangement that the commissioning party (the woman and her
husband) and Ledare finally arrived at stated that Ledare would
create a work for his artistic use and public exhibition from
the photographic session, and a private edition of seven black
and whites for the sitter, whose identity would be protected
and unidentified. Like *Double Bind*, the photographing that
occurred between July 22–July 28, 2011, from a week-long
stay on the part of Ledare at the couple's home, was realized
collaboratively. The images that resulted may not ultimately
have conformed to or affirmed the commissioner's earliest
intentions. The public edition incorporates seven photographs
made with the sitter, one per day. In the photographic images,
the sitter's face is redacted and each image appears as an inset
within an enlarged *New York Times* front page. Handwritten
passages in pencil on black paper by Ledare are also placed
within the frame. The public edition also includes a redacted
version of the legal contract that defined the terms of the
agreement from which the work was generated and describes
each parties' rights and limitations for usage for the private
and public editions. The seven-page contract printed in
archival LaserJet is presented in a vitrine. *An Invitation* was
first exhibited at Pilar Corrias Gallery, London, May 24–
June 21, 2012.

6.   The *Ephemera* magazines—a sequence of six numbered
magazines totaling 479 pages—comprise the last of the *Double
Bind* publication's three volumes. Within a unique installation
version of *Ephemera* that Ledare first exhibited at Michèle
Didier's gallery in Paris, each page of these magazines
was printed as a poster. These posters were then collectively
arranged in a grid that lined the walls of the space and stretched
from floor to ceiling. The remaining two volumes of the
publication—a book called *Husbands* that catalogued every
single image made on the two trips, and a book called *Diptychs*,
which reproduced all of the wall works (in other words, each
diptych as well as the singular photographs, which in this
instance were included as inserts)—were presented in vitrines
or on tables. The idea of this installation was to invert the
hierarchy of importance, thus placing greater visual emphasis on
the mass-media imagery as opposed to the private performances,
or at least to suggest something of the differing levels of
intimacy in encountering these distinct registers of the piece.

V

RHEA ANASTAS : What other influences from viewing or reading are important to locate from this time?

> LEIGH LEDARE : There was a very important text for me that Eric de Bruyn published in 2006, "Topological Pathways of Post-Minimalism," that discussed in depth the work of Dan Graham and Stanley Brouwn as related to postminimalism and the ideas of topology initially proposed by the psychologist Kurt Lewin in the thirties.[7]

Was Lewin already using the term topology?

> He was definitely using it, taking these dynamic and spatial concepts from the field of topological geometry, and applying them to social psychology, as a kind of extension of Gestalt therapy. A number of artists, Graham and Bruce Nauman among them, had major interest in topology. My grandfather had known Lewin, and also Erving Goffman, and would talk to my brother and me about some of their concepts when we were adolescents. He actually used those ideas to abstract and explain some of the rather complex dynamics within our own family, to allow us to reframe our situation through the reasoned social systems these models provided. Funny enough, when I came across de Bruyn's piece I started realizing just how important some of these ideas had been to ways that I'd been dealing with the content and structure of my own work up to that point.

> The amazing thing about topology is that rather than primarily recording static things, it records dynamic relations. You can plug any set of actual relations into an abstract topological model—similar to the way that the abstract model of the script in *Double Bind* allows for specific relations to be recorded. By seeing relations as constantly in flux, there's an ongoing variability in positions and movements. One cliché image that accompanies topology is the Möbius strip: the inside becomes the outside, only to then become the inside once more. This figure of culture, intersubjective relations, and the psyche contains something labyrinthine.

These ideas have to do with the spatial description of the object, or subject. What would the subject's conditions be?

> I'm talking about a psychosocial field within which multiple subjects and objects exist in dynamic relation. It's a graphing of that field, not from a singular objective perspective, but from one understood to be composing itself from the inside out, subjectively experienced from any specific entity within the field of relations. It concerns dynamics at the level of the individual and the group. In a topological model, that field and the subjects within it are constantly in a process of both being formed and forming the space and relations around them. The theory allows for different dynamics of intersubjectivity. It begins with the notion of the boundary that separates a subject from the world around them, to understand influence as a product of how enclosed, or porous, that boundary may be. Influence presents itself in degrees: it can be symmetric or asymmetric. Essentially, starting with two entities, one entity may be much more susceptible to influence than the other.

Intersubjectivity is really fundamental then. Topology seems to allow for something that's about the relationship between people and things, as objects.

> Also, temporal dimensions are not fixed in a topological model— the past can fold back into the present. That can also re-present influence. Different temporal spaces, or relations to reality or fantasy, can exist simultaneously, one plane mapped over another. This is especially useful in thinking about group dynamics, and the complex corridors from one perspective to another.

What other ideas from the core principles of topology should we describe?

> Well, I picked up on how topology conceptualizes different scales of the self: the singular self, the dyadic self, the triadic self, group identity, and cultural or historical identity, for instance. The self is defined through differentiation. But we also intersubjectively

define the self through our merging with others, and through the stories and roles we identify with and use to navigate these relations. Topology foregrounds this notion of interdependence or connectedness. There are different degrees of connectedness, influence, or identification. For instance, you might have a very high degree that relates to a reciprocal encounter with another individual, like sexual attraction, which is always mediated by the interior psychological experience of one's own past. Or you might have a very low degree that relates to an onlooker in a crowd of onlookers staring at something, where all in the crowd are experiencing this event, but from disconnected angles. These are two distinct points on a spectrum of what we could look at as viewership models, meaning being contingent on what each of those viewers brings to their observation and how active or passive their engagement is.

So a period of reading some of this work on topology preceded working on *Double Bind*?

For sure. There were other texts I was reading as well: Deleuze's *Difference and Repetition*; also, Kaja Silverman, her *Male Subjectivity at the Margins*—an analysis of masochism in Fassbinder's films—as well as her book *World Spectators*, which dealt with phenomenological issues around ontology and subjectivity. Plus Silverman's book *Flesh of my Flesh* . . . There she advocated the creation of analog models, emphasizing subjectivity and empathy as vehicles for reorienting that which gets positioned as culturally irreconcilable, or othered in some sense. Her position started from what, for her, constituted an ethics of looking and engagement. The idea was to overcome some of the impasses that have been a side effect of the divisiveness of identity politics. She stressed the crucial role art and ontology might play in providing spaces of agonism, where similarity can be acknowledged while still accounting for difference and even the pluralistic, irreconcilable condition of things. Most importantly, though, I'd emphasize my listening to the cultural materials and structures, even being open to a situation presenting itself.

Turning back to the de Bruyn article, it offers an alternative to the dominant Euclidian geometric model of the ocular. De Bruyn's models are Brouwn, but also a Merleau-Ponty text, *The Visible and the Invisible*, for its description of an immediate "wild" being in perception. Outside and inside are crossed. Boundaries between subject and object are indeterminate, somewhat akin to the mother-child relational views of psychoanalysis. This is a preperspectival vision, associated with the child and a primordial past, when the visual field is mixed, variously directed by a body, not yet shaped by a learned, universalized vision alone.

De Bruyn's narration reads differently than the routine claims about art since 1968. This builds in a viewpoint that is uneven across time—that is, in terms of how the artwork is said to respond to the political pressures of its moment. Rather than statements of mastery, tactical moves on a different scale and different notions than directional ones come forward. Similarly, complicated movements within reception and temporal dimensions may now enter into the story . . .

> For a critically engaged artist to call attention to a set of issues, to not just say "look at this," but to say *how* to look at it, that's something different than a mannered espousing of criticality. This has to be evaluated through an artist's investment and long-standing critical engagement. It doesn't happen simply by showing at a specific venue, or referencing someone else's ideas, but has more to do with developing an attitude. If the work engages critically, then as viewers we're asked to carry that *expectation* forward, to look at what the artist is guiding us to look at. Still, there's no guarantee this won't be flawed.

And no guarantee that any criticism of the work won't also be flawed in its ways of considering that positioning! I can easily get exasperated about these problematics. But let me just say, I think that one of the most frequent ways claims-based criticism does this is to take that expectation to be critical in a fixed or stable way, in an is-or-isn't, success-or-failure scenario. I think that word *expectation* is a very powerful idea for criticism to take responsibility for: what

the beholder brings. This is surely related to what you've said about
the "how" of looking, and this attention to the bridge of expectation
and responsibility, even ethics, between artist or work and viewer.

> In *Double Bind*, but also in a topological model, authority and
> authorship are decentered but not denied. This puts forward an
> interrelational model of subjectivity—although, like we discussed,
> I'm already borrowing and applying an existing set of cultural
> systems, these particular relationships or positions that we're
> ascribed to.

> In this sense, topology coincides with the enactment model that
> we were talking about, in that it allows a field to be staged that
> becomes a site of experimentation—it applies pressure in order
> to diagram and spatialize this experimental site. I think in both
> the early video-art movements, and in the group-psychology
> ones, there was a lot of thought that, through informationalizing
> the space of intersubjective relations, a collective would be able
> to deduce what is and isn't working, and consequently better
> understand the dynamics at play underneath these situations, and
> then be able to allow productive feedback to reenter in order to
> improve the functioning of social relations or society.

I get the feeling that you pull and extend these philosophical models
and conceptual frameworks into being about the ocular, about
seeing, because you want the ocular to serve you in a lot of other
ways than it has done within your inheritance as a photographer.
Though it's not about a notion of correctness—I think the mapping
of these theoretical models is interestingly imperfect: highly useful
and functional, on the one hand, and ultimately tenuous as logical or
verbal constructions, on the other hand, because the ideas are being
put to use in the process of *Double Bind*.

> That nonfidelity is important. It's also what we're doing with
> this conversation: applying ideas, examining them, and actually
> *looking*. Our opinions might shift too.

I could think of you coming off of *Pretend You're Actually Alive*, trying to work against an association with expressive photography. Let's say you want to show us that in fact there's a very different conceptual apparatus operating in the work.

> These ideas are a part of the lineage of my development as an artist, which speaks to the kinds of work I gravitated toward and was exposed to, not to mention conversations that developed in line with new concerns that my work presented for me as it went deeper. Yes, I grew up how I grew up, belonging to a specific family and within a certain moment. But later I lived in New York, went to RISD, and then attended Columbia for an MFA. While there I was reading many theorists, and working closely with people like Gareth James. James was also associated with the gallery projects Orchard and Reena Spaulings, spaces where I met Guagnini and John Kelsey, among others. Also at Columbia were Kara Walker, Jutta Koether, John Miller, and Collier Schorr, as well as all sorts of artists and thinkers who were visitors to Columbia, lecturing and coming to studios at the time: Elizabeth Grosz, Andrea Fraser, and Taussig (who taught in another department). It's interesting for me to reflect on these interactions—Grosz's book *Volatile Bodies*, with its subtitle "Towards a Corporal Feminism," was one instance in which a feminist critic was trying to problematize what she saw as an impasse in feminist critiques. For me, there was also a way I was trying to question, somewhat irreverently or against certain authorities, the things I found myself implicated in, taking up all these ideas and belief structures and testing them against others.

There are genealogies, families we choose, and there are the families we have. It's struck me in thinking about *Double Bind* the extent to which your relationships are materials and, I guess, points from which to create and generate ideas. To say that is not at all to say that your work is personal in the way that descriptor is typically understood. I am speaking from a location that's in line with feminist critiques and the feminism of my practice—a criticism built of a rigorous consideration of materiality, psychology, experience.

> That's also where being in conversation with other artists and their work, artists such as Mike Kelley, Paul McCarthy, or Andrea

Fraser, comes in. On one level, you can never actually understand the culture you come from until you've sounded it out, until you've pushed at it and seen how it responds, and how you respond in turn. And on another, once you've experienced shifts, once you've experienced another culture or another viewpoint in enough depth, you can't necessarily return to the same beliefs you held to earlier either. Your prior understandings are bracketed—they shift, they expand.

What I mean to say is that the personal is also interrelational. We're marked by all these things, our families, social class, cultural backgrounds, educations, and subjective experiences. Certain aspects of my position are deeply embedded within my work, while other aspects are also called into conflict by it. Moreover, the work intervenes in these earlier identifications, complicating them and making it necessary to redefine my position in relation to these transforming relations, and to reapproach them with nuance and a continued questioning. It's almost like fieldwork, an education that keeps unfolding, and at times this can be ambivalent, posing conflicts that erupt and test earlier-held beliefs. No one's life experience comes down to their CV, nor does anyone's work speak about everything; not at all. And there's a lot that simply can't be defined—the questions that have to do with how and why we come to pursue what we pursue in our lives. Nevertheless, I am interested in how the stuff of subjective experience is interwoven within so many other structures. This sense of distinction between the two is another false binary, one that I'm trying to call into question.

7.   Eric de Bruyn, "Topological Pathways of Post-Minimalism," *Grey Room* 25 (Fall 2006): 32–63.

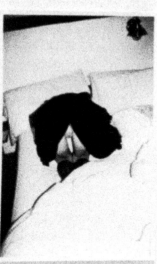

LAST ADDRESS AND EQUIVALENT IMAGE
[unreadable]
No. 3.0.3 — Le séance de chantal du jour
[unreadable] ng. Parti, press de Madrid

VI.

LEIGH LEDARE : The emphasis on subjectivity and psychology makes me not only want to draw our attention to how *Double Bind* produces or frames affect, but what strikes me as a more important question: How does *Double Bind* utilize affect as a raw material, and how does it direct affect and give it a new positioning? In other words, within the structure of *Double Bind*, what does affect—as a catalyst—produce?

RHEA ANASTAS : What do you mean by *catalyst*? And by speaking of directing affect, of tactical uses of it? The body-mind takes in and responds, being in enjoyment, being in sexual attraction . . .

What I mean is that affect draws us into this sensory intensity which compels, but which can also function like a trap. It can be harnessed and framed, directed to push us around. It can overwhelm what might be seen as reasonable, and is nothing if not contagious, which is also why it's experienced as so troubling to control.

So, once we've acknowledged that, what then, on a macro level, does the entire enactment and staging of *Double Bind* serve up to the viewer? And if it does stage a negative affect, how might *Double Bind* as an object, loaded as it is, act on the viewer, and on the expectations of the social milieu against which it is staged? How might it be received by the viewer only to be othered? Or how might it mirror back the viewer's own investments in mirroring the social? Even if as a viewer you are positioned outside, *Double Bind* centers you on these relations, breaking down that boundary and immersing the viewer inescapably inside. Maybe you can speak to how you experience this?

I think we have to leave the structure of *Double Bind*—that is, leave the question of what you're calling the tactical negotiation of the performers aside for a moment—and leave the question of what the object of the affect may be. Affect is distinguished from behavior in psychology, and is well-positioned as a counter to many of the understandings in the fields of psychology that are directional, from inputs and outputs, from Freudian psychology and its repression/liberation binary. It's what Sedgwick, in her study of Silvan Tomkins's midcentury theory of affect, outlines as the "self-validating" quality of affect (Tomkins's terminology): it's layered in Sedgwick's view, and comes through the spectrum of objects that affects seize upon. The distinction that Sedgwick locates through Tomkins's theory is the difference between this set of physiologically rooted attractions, irritations, and other connections, and the language-based idea of referentiality (familiar from our notion of "theory").[8]

I can use this to reframe my viewing in section I, and in this sense your way of referring to affect as the raw material of response is apt. There is my liking and not liking to be looked at in my own mind and body, and the type of liking that I see in the images of Meghan that differs from mine, the enjoyment there and the alienated feeling, or even an angry frustration. I like to talk and to have my talking heard by another—by you, for one—and I may not see that reflected in the images of Meghan; it's blocked from the viewer. I am speaking about the images now and the way that I spoke of them in section I, which was through my emotions and my projection of myself into them, which is distinct from a structuralist theory–based perspective, intellectualized and distanced, or a language-based framing.

Further, affect allows the consideration of fear and also shame. Both strike me as majorly important to the response mechanics your work treats. Shame arises within the responses of excitement or interest that have been brought up. Sedgwick makes a really fascinating distinction within Tomkins's thought about shame being described through the strange as opposed to the prohibited or disapproved, undercutting the repression model with this more affect-based "indifferent" positioning toward the object of stimulation. My impulse is to address this as an excess. There is the serial introduction of the viewer—a placing of the viewer into contact with images and performances that might bring excitement, fear, or pleasure, in an intensified way—and there is the density of the work's material, repetition, scale.

But that excessive quality of affect, that kind of intensity and insistence it carries—as viewers, it works on us, not the other way around. This intensity creates a fissure that threatens to make us the object of its drama, one that begs us to fall inside. That fissure nominates us as subjects; it encounters us, implicates us, forces us to position ourselves.

This makes me consider the outcome had Meghan and Adam refused to participate in *Double Bind*. Having expressed this loaded request, and having revealed a certain insistence of my desire, as ambiguous as it might be, would still leave behind a residue. Affect calls forward an excess, which once exposed cannot be taken back. It can reerupt, which is partly what *Double Bind* initiates. I want to insist that the unbearable quality of this excess is always intersubjective, always about—as Lauren Berlant and Lee Edelman suggest in their dialogue on intercourse, both as sex and conversation, in *Sex, or the Unbearable*—an encounter. In other words, we are made contingent to this encounter. It may be mobilized socially to necessitate a decision, while revealing that indecision is also a decision. Yet maybe emphasizing intersubjectivity is misleading. Perhaps we need to locate this as a quality of estrangement: the subject is forced to reconcile this strangeness, not in sight of the other but, leading circuitously through the other, to themselves.

With the sexual encounters in *Double Bind*, the gap between the participants' feelings and experiences and the viewer's is large; it's in a certain sense unbridgeable.

Here's where I want to hold the layers apart from each other. You in some sense revisit (through enactment, repetition) a past sexual pathway within your relationship with Meghan. You do this as a work. You conceive and direct things, you are looking through the camera, and you are aware of making images with Meghan—and later combining these with other images.

In saying this, I had a flash of insight. Something that you spoke about earlier, and that I may not have been able to understand, is just this: your insistence on a language of absence, or a displacement of photographic seeing, within your images of Meghan. Maybe you are speaking from producing within that space of feeling, where you have scripted an artwork, one that has you facing a past experience?

> Well, I'm never only one or the other. In each instance I happen to be both, which might be to say that I want it both ways. And this may not be unrelated to the way *Double Bind* stages a crisis around identification. But in regards to your comment, one of my points, one of my reasons for tethering the image to these interrelational structures, has been to emphasize the way that underlying these images there's always a kind of ecology of relations, with feedback, duration, and contingency each involved. The dominant ideas about photographs and the indexical sign have this way of overemphasizing a linguistic model for representation and assuming that meaning begins and ends with the visible, or that the visible is a position of authority—when there is all that can't be seen, the limitations of the symbolic, etc.

I have to amplify something within your slippery positioning of being "both." Your methods include using yourself—a first-person, autobiographical model. Yes, I am going to use that prohibited paradigm. I have my own reasons for doing that—a curiosity about undoing the dominant subject-is-performative, subject-is-language-and-culture, no-biology-or-naturalized-identities-allowed doxa of the structuralist/poststructuralist world, right? How can we view your role otherwise, because part of that "both" is being yourself in your life in the piece, and also being a participant in an artwork that uses some relationships in your life? The viewer has no vantage on where the one can be split from the other. To say it's all performative is to do something damaging to the narrative, to the actually felt, and to the risky model of acting and creating through these mixed concretes and symbolics in your work.

> Through our self-objectification we each in relation to the others become signifiers, signified, and signifying agents, and all this positioning happens amidst an excess that is impossible to disentangle.

The intersubjectivity is misleading in this moment. I'm not sure that we can argue it this way, as if to say being inside your work, having an encounter with your work, is raw emotion. But we should try to work through what the work may allow . . . A form of cognitive access, a line or a pathway to a language of affect?

The moves toward and away from affect, and the self-validating structure of affect for the subject, suggest to me that we have to try to find the contours of the spaces the viewer inhabits in your work, and these may put the viewer in a position that is very different and untheoretical compared to that of most critical art, where representation is largely assumed to happen through language. Emotions are the raw materials, not quite representations. And yet the work also has a representational and a structural layer.

> Let's talk about what you suggested a couple minutes ago—in particular, that your visceral response wells up from what the work's structure denies, those same dynamics and containments the work enacts in order that, paradoxically, they might be encircled and made present . . . those blocks of Meghan's voice, for one. But we could also look at this problem of the commodity—how my appropriation of labor within the production of *Double Bind* foregrounds the conventions of authorship and the management/expropriation of surplus. Mirroring back at us a set of uncanny dilemmas that produce a negative affect in turn, *Double Bind's* enactment might be more destabilizing than we'd expect, for the reason that this acknowledgment threatens to shatter an optimism we have to hold onto in order to participate cleanly within the social. As individuals we'd like to believe that we're autonomous; however, it's through the social that we gauge the parameters for how to behave ethically or morally. As individuals not only is our own subjective judgment susceptible to bad judgment—one reason why we defer to higher authorities, offering ourselves up as their subjects—but obviously the foundations of broader cultural values can rest on bad judgment. When you describe affect as "indifferent," I still think of how affect can be put toward these controls. I consider how belief is regulated through the social, how it is naturalized as truth—in other words, as true to the interests of

a given position. This intensity of the emotional, a kind of "reason beyond reason," anchors these mechanics of control, but it can also loosen, threatening the rational underpinnings of the s ocial order, where it is typically cast as antisocial. I also don't think we can lose sight of how historically gendered these dichotomies are, how strongly they've favored attributes of the masculine. I want to suggest that affects underlie beliefs, but also that other affects can trouble beliefs—we shouldn't forget that once a belief becomes codified, its believers are called on to defend it as an exclusive truth.

If *Double Bind*'s staging of contradictions and excess messes with beliefs, negates or threatens to undercut them, it's not in order to cynically dismiss any belief, or to replace one belief with another, but to ask how a given belief is applied and what its application means; what it conceals or closes off, how the social pressure maintaining this belief may try to force us to go along whole cloth, even blindly. The point of *Double Bind* is to bring this crisis to a boil, where we have to individuate our positions, whatever those might be. This is where recognizing difference becomes crucial. Negation is also always coupled with this excess, which persistently threatens to interrupt the sovereignty of any singular position or subject. So the double bind could be sited on numerous levels—at the level of discourse, or the viewer or participants, or even within our conversation.

I want to hear more about how you are figuring social participation in this context.

All aspects of the social exploit affect. We might consider how affect is harnessed as the engine for political participation, or how deeply it underwrites our commitment to the social or familial. It's indistinguishable from the emotionally and physically felt stakes that underlie all our social codes and beliefs. I might add, we're often completely unaware of its working on us—why, for instance, we feel the conviction to make one decision over another. I say this even though affect might extort something from the viewer, by drawing on needs, wishes, and satisfactions.

Let's talk about your role. You are the structuralist, giving shape to the scripting and the layers of social and cultural complexity and intersubjectivity in the work. But maybe these languages aren't the only thing. Given your work with your mother in *Pretend*, your identification with Meghan, and the intimacy in those photographs you and Meghan took, this feels actual and private. You're more implicated than most narrators, and what you've created and what it sets in motion in *Double Bind* and *Pretend* make me wonder if structuralist, deconstructive critiques and assumptions about these orthodoxies still hold, and if they can still be potent—I mean the linguistic model for analyzing representation and especially photographs.

> That brings us back once again to this either/or impasse that I believe rests on a series of false binaries. Actually, contrary to how I can intellectualize it, I experience these aspects of the structural and personal as impossibly intertwined—they're nested in each other, and are products of each other. Together they form a knot that can't be unraveled. To attempt to do so is to be left simply holding a single strand that no longer resembles the complexity of the original object. What *Double Bind* tries to do, and I think how together we've tried to approach this conversation, is to slice and cross-cut this tangle of issues, discourses, and positions in various ways.

That's what I wanted to do, by making this move that I can't actually pull off, but wanted to point to. That's what I mean by speaking about your sexual encounter with Meghan in the terms of affect and in a way that is not yet a symbolization, not yet a representation. There's a certain sense in which for the viewer, from the outside, that affective image becomes symbol, when seen from that vantage.

> There is a complexifying relation, to be sure. For me what you just described falls into one of the places where interrelationality complicates that which had been seen or comprehended through the indexical.

It interests me that your work has these layers or passages in which symbolization doesn't occur, and here teleological assumptions and directional lines of surface and depth, and figure and ground, may be avoided.

But it would require you to own the affective spaces and hold back from making cultural meanings out of them—this is the extension of the self-validating description of affect, it's outside the frameworks based upon referentiality. The whole human thing is cultural, of course, but in that passage (what to call it?) of *Double Bind*, there might not be a telling or information about culture that is produced.

Are you an antistructuralist or a lapsed one? Can we think of *Double Bind* as enacting your crisis with the structures and critical models derived from this theory?

Or to approach it from the opposite angle: perhaps *Double Bind* is attempting to redress that overemphasis on affect so prevalent within certain traditions of photography. So much of that production simply seems to bleed into itself, overemphasizing the visual and the framing of the ocular, a collecting or grabbing of emotions and affects that are ultimately pointless, that pronounce their existence simply for the sake of themselves, without reflection on the act of framing or the broader ways these framings might be framed—this has always left me wanting. Counter to this, the kind of poiesis that's constituted by enactment—what Niklas Luhmann refers to as autopoiesis—isn't any simple repetition. Rather, it's the creation of a system that constitutes its own product, where the operation is the condition for the production of further operations. It's a system that continues to shift and unfold, whether we're talking about a feedback mechanism or reception. This is in part what enactment facilitates, approaching the structural through an application of the personal and affective, socially and intersubjectively. It doesn't illustrate; it embodies. In articulating a theorization of affect, we have to be careful not to cut out the social. We can't exclude a performative model, this Foucaultian model, or even a structural/linguistic model. This is where someone like Taussig's theorization of the negative, his insistence on exactly how this affect underlies the contractual movements of the social, becomes so important, how discourses act in self-interested ways to authorize singular perspectives as truth. Here is also where it's important to define that notion of excess, or the gap.

I have the sense that this has been the source of some of the ways that *Double Bind* feels hard to locate conceptually and as a set of representations—it being both of and potentially transformative and negating to those tropes of photographic imagery and its readings. Maybe key is the (negative) reading that the work performs.

> Maybe this also lies in how it situates itself as an archive and as a complex system, one that foregrounds this very contradictory positioning and resists being utilized toward a positivistic end.

And that emotion and expressions are in fact explored, rather than being disallowed.

> Yes, and that too!

And then there are the models that haven't yet been conceptualized, the gaps between what might be attributed to viewing *Double Bind* and what may lie in considering it in other ways—materially, in cultural or social terms, and in context. I am sympathetic to the multiplicity, and the unfixing of one model over another. But my aims in having this dialogue, in doing this conceptual work together, well, I've been holding onto a question or contradiction—a conflict—about how *Double Bind* can be read to uphold structuralist symbolizations, and I have also been asking myself all along if the opposite weren't also true, that politics and agency aren't actually located in the symbolic. We have these received models of criticism still very much in use today which are so assured in their arguments about the politics of art and cultural objects as opposed to the politics of activism. I have my doubts about whether present-day theory really has such a convincing purchase on either, or that the two are opposed . . . There is an assuredness to writing today that reads political or critical art as tragic, failed; that seems to project or gain authority through the pronouncement of failure and pessimism, and in an elusive origin in history.

When Andrea Fraser and I and others were working on Orchard, we discussed these assumptions, and in her article on Michael Asher, I recall her using the term "euphemized" to talk about the real investments in material decisions, production, research, and exchanges with institutions; she was referring to how writing about Asher's practice minimized so many elements of the practice in the service of theorizations about its criticality.[9] That's just one example of many.

> We clearly have to realize that just because something names itself as political, or is named as critical, or whatever, that doesn't in and of itself constitute a politics. Its categorization can just as easily be a misnomer, can claim too much or cut other things out.

In this dialogue, we have been resolutely empirical, using observation, description, testing, etc. We've been on a search for what the work holds in all its layers—the material, the abstract, the language based, the corporeal, the cultural. We've also been enacting, using ourselves and implicating ourselves, as you and the others do in *Double Bind*. My investment has been in exposing my investments—also, using them to understand how the authorities and routinizations of theory close off considerations that are risky, or contain and predetermine learning that we need to pursue, that is urgent.

> That seems to resonate with Moten and Stefano Harney's idea of study, black study. *Study* is something altogether different than the situation of being a student, being at a university, which is systemic and passive. It's what the subject can do that may not be authorized.

Following on what I just said, that my investment has been in exposing my investments, I want to know how that corresponds to your ideas about how conceptualizing can be, how you want it to be. How would you describe this dialogue, as viewing and thinking?

Well, again, I think this dialogue is about that encounter. In a sense, it's been a process of your pressing on me, acting on me, and a back and forth between us, me acting on you, which itself parallels how I'm acting on the viewer. I also see what I'm doing as a productive intervention, a kind of parasiting function where as a variable *(x)* I stimulate an existing situation in order to sound out what variable *(y)* is. You turn that back around on me, pressing me and sounding out my position. I see this as congruent with a feminist mode of inquiry, where it's about creating a revelation so that if you choose to participate in the thing, not that you have a choice, then you have to participate consciously.

We've been really fixated on testing out what can be done with two voices in a back-and-forth conversation, within this encounter. And to use *encounter* is to describe a relational space that changes, and, as you say, is susceptible to varying responses that will affect the verbal surface of things. This commitment to an empiricism or praxis, and to difference—both of these I relate to feminist critiques of language, and the very difficult reaching for nondualistic forms of thought. This has meant to test out a process of working with concepts and theory differently than in the norms of singly-authored texts and the habitual, routine uses of contemporary theory in my field. It marks a searching and a doubt about the kinds of authorities usually invested in writing, and also doubts about the primacy of language and verbal forms.

The dialogue allows us to move into and voice those areas of experience in viewing, and in the whole array of nonverbal phenomena that are often separated and dominated by the privileging of the verbal and the language based. Or at least to locate their edges and to locate our telling in a less vertical (surface/depth, figure/ground) way.

Can our work be serious, thorough, consistent, and somehow avoid models of analysis that are overwhelmingly linguistic and structural? Can we use this encounter to loosen the pairings that our relative positions could just as easily be performed, to different aims, to uphold—writer and artist, producer and receiver, verbalizing the nonverbal?

When you describe it this way, I'm struck by just how much this dialogue also parallels the production of *Double Bind*, starting with what it means for each of us as participants to take on that risk, to engage in this encounter, to sound out those relations, recording and presenting them, and finally listening, reflecting, studying them, producing discourse. The amount of work it takes to do this is surprising, and it's much easier to hide, to not comment, to not place oneself on the line, to not be self-reflective in the ways we're forcing each other to be—or in the case of the artist's conventional relationship to the critic's role, to leave that for someone else to do. I think, however, that the self-theorization folded into *Double Bind*, coupled with its intensely personal material, makes this nearly impossible. In some sense this book is an attempt at distilling that. For me this book, rather than being a reading of the work, is also a continuation of the work. It makes me wonder what responsibility I have as a performer to continue performing the work—to be there for the conversations that are to be had.

The process of making *Double Bind*, and the process of reflection around the piece—around its relations and two distinct trips, its dialogue between private images and experiences and those public forms of address that the media images pronounce, the comparative structuring that orders this complex dialogue internal to the piece—is initiated through the performances and that material field only to pivot onto this discursive conversation.

The sex in *Double Bind*—representations of it and the senses of it—is a shifting terrain. It drifts through the work onto good and bad objects, right? Someone else's Meghan; the media's or porn magazines' telling of sex, and offering of objects to use to produce it; the acts of photography and scopophilic looking; your and Adam's looking, and the viewer's. Things are refracted and threaded-through, somehow not private or contained.

If I want to be really honest, it's necessary for me to admit to what extent I might be psychically invested in these situations, in their outcomes, the positions they script, even the problems they put forward—my desires, my anxieties around the photographic act, my place within the interrelations, even blocks I myself might have and be blind to, and also that perversity of play and humor that erupt inside the work. Despite the vulnerability that can come through identifying myself with something as extremely difficult to recognize as this, I still can't pretend that I'm exempt. It's necessary for me to look at all this too. It's necessary for all of us to look at ourselves. To treat this all as some intellectual exercise and completely deny complicity or the movements of the psyche, to rationally frame all these problems away, that would seem extremely false.

On the other hand, I'm highly aware of how I mark myself in revealing all this, how I become susceptible to critique, to being messed with in turn. What I've found, however, is that the vulnerability that comes with this also shifts the conversation, allowing the work to get under the skin, to get places that we might otherwise not be able.

One means of locating a difference between sexual difference as a set of contradictions under patriarchy, and sexuality in *Double Bind* more broadly, is to ask you to speak about the invested, complicit position you perform in some respects in the work: being the ex-husband of Meghan, shooting with her, and through her with Adam, creating these images; sharing your fixation on the way sexuality and the sexual revolution plays out in such intense ways in the imagery of the media collection.

Look, it's not about me perpetuating something, but rather framing something that's already there in the only way possible: to create a model of it, and to invest it with the stakes of actually performing the very thing I'm criticizing. To say, "Look, it's in me too."

There is a caginess in this. How does the self-revelation of intentions for each of us in the work, and for the viewer, play out? And what does this mean when my intentions are also to destabilize and create a flux of meaning, to undo what's known? This is to place intentions outside of one's control and to undergo something—something experimental.

This is what the self-implicating position of complicity
brings forward . . .

> It's hugely important to keep open the possibility of articulating
> these feminist concerns from the position of a male subject, as the
> male subject is also firmly implicated within them.

Aren't all of us implicated? Female and male, queer and other. I
think it can't be a dualism.

I want to return to an idea of feminist interventions within
knowledge, to experience or praxis and knowledge in an absolutely
nonpositivistic sense. One benefit to my own "wrongness," that
shifting or correctable aspect, is that I am learning, and the ideas
we put forward are incomplete. In being deliberate about this
learning, in the modest position I take within this dialogue, and
within collaborating with you, the door is open. It's crucial how
changeable the process of knowing and using that knowing and its
identifications and relationships is made to be in viewing *Double
Bind*, and in viewing all art that reaches us complexly and deeply.

It's like Meghan's position as actor, witness, and photographed
object/image, and like her position within the couples—or yours
or Adam's, for that matter. Any half of the couple is in this way an
equal half of the relational entity or whole. It's composed, shaped
within the piece. It's incomplete. It depends on the moves made by
others. Selfhood is a thing we may only grasp in the fragmentary
ways it's mirrored back to us, or in the act of producing images
or writing or reading. The grasping of value within the process is
a questioning of value. Or, conversely, we may grasp it best in the
moments of high theater, irony, perversion. It's the writer's/artist's
problem of moving from interiority to the exterior.

> It's extremely lazy and limiting to presume that these structural
> binaries (as useful as they are) are not overdetermining, that they
> can be taken as law, that a male subject couldn't also occupy a
> position of lack, or identify with the concerns stemming from a
> feminist line of inquiry, or a queer cross-cutting of this.

Even if we are speaking outside of intention-based models, we are still opening up the operations of the work according to each of our responses as well as those of Meghan and Adam. How does this conversation have to be understood as situated inside this problem of destabilization, of incompleteness, of testing where value lies? We are still in the place of irresolution. We are still talking about messing things up, and messing things up further.

Saying that, I also have to recognize my own naïveté, where I might also be wrong about certain things, simply unaware, or more complexly, uncertain. Or more crucially, I have to recognize where the conversation might be extended or doubled-back on by others—by viewers of *Double Bind* and by readers of this book.

8.   See Eve Kosofsky Sedgwick, *Touching Feeling: Affect, Pedagogy, Performativity* (Durham & London: Duke University Press, 2003), 100.

9.   Andrea Fraser, "Procedural Matters: The Art of Michael Asher," *Artforum* 46, no. 10 (Summer 2008): 374–381.

Unlimited at Art Basel
Art Basel (Gianni Jetzer, curator)
June 15–21, 2015

Leigh Ledare
Mitchell-Innes & Nash, New York
March 21–April 26, 2014

Leigh Ledare, et. al.
Kunsthal Charlottenborg, Copenhagen (Stine Hebert, curator)
January 18–May 12, 2013

Leigh Ledare, et. al.
WIELS Contemporary Art Centre, Brussels (Elena Filipovic, curator)
September 8–December 2, 2012

Double Bind Publication
Michèle Didier, Paris
September 13–November 10, 2012

Leigh Ledare
The Box, Los Angeles
March 7–April 21, 2012

How Soon is Now
The Garage Center for Contemporary Art, Moscow (Beatrix Ruf, Tom Eccles, Hans Ulrich Obrist, Philippe Parreno, and Liam Gillick, curators)
November 20, 2010–February 28, 2011

Prix Découverte, Les Rencontres d'Arles
Les Rencontres d'Arles, Arles (Beatrix Ruf, Tom Eccles, Hans Ulrich Obrist, Philippe Parreno, and Liam Gillick, curators)
July 3–September 19, 2010